THINK DOG!

THINK DOG!

An Owner's Guide to Canine Psychology

John Fisher

Trafalgar Square Publishing

NORTH POMFRET, VERMONT

First published in the United States of America in 1991
by Trafalgar Square Publishing, North Pomfret, Vermont 05053.

© John Fisher 1990

The right of John Fisher to be identified as
author of this work has been asserted by him
in accordance with the Copyright Designs and
Patents Act 1988

Library of Congress Catalog Card Number: 91-65570
ISBN: 0 943955 46 7

Acknowledgements:

The cartoons in Chapter 3 are by Michael Bunnage.
The author and publisher also wish to thank
David Shaw and the publishers of *Pet Product
Marketing* for permission to use the article
on pages 85 to 88.

Printed and Bound in the United States of America

Dedicated to my parents, who find it difficult trying to explain to people what I do for a living, to my wife Liz whose encouragement has got me this far and to my son Jason who always wanted to have his name in a book.

Contents

Introduction

Tell me a friend who is more true,
a guide to light my path,
or wicked rogue with honest heart,
and eyes that touch my soul.
Honoured by an early King
and favoured by a queen.
In work who is an artist,
at sport does reign supreme.
The guardian of my family,
our stock he doth protect,
and tho' he's only very small
He earned the world's respect.

Michael Gillow

This tribute to the dog nicely sums up the admiration that millions of people feel for this animal with whom they share their homes. "A guide to light my path," makes one immediately think of the guide dog leading a blind person. "In work who is an artist," suggests the Border Collie bringing in the sheep. "Guardian of my family, our stock he doth protect," conjures up pictures of the German Shepherd Dog protecting our homes, or the Old English Sheepdog watching over our flocks.

Because dogs are capable of performing all of these tasks and many more besides, we tend to take the view that we understand them and that they understand the job of work that we want them to perform. But do we really understand dogs? I suspect that we do not. What is more to the point, do dogs understand us? Again, I suspect the answer is no.

If we were to stand back and examine the dog for what it is, we would realise how silly it is to place human values on the things they do – and examining the dog, for what it really is, is what this book is all about. If we can understand more about dogs, what motivates them, what their values are, how they learn and why they do what they do, then this greater understanding will help us to form a more enjoyable relationship with them.

Sadly at the moment good caring owners are being given bad advice. A while ago I reviewed a book in which it was stated that a thin bamboo cane should be used to hit the dog on the muzzle if it tried to walk in front of you. It also said that to stop a dog accepting bribes from strangers you should put a pin in a piece of meat: the pin should stick out about half an inch and, as the dog noses forward, the pin will prick it slightly. Alternatively, the same exercise can be carried out with a fork, which will also prick the dog's outstretched mouth and prevent it from swallowing the food. On the front cover of the book is the name of an august and influential body of people within the dog world, although on investigation they proved to have had nothing to do with it. It is a very flashy looking book and it is reasonably priced. My derogatory review was never printed, and the book is available in bookshops and libraries. What chance does the caring pet owner have, if this is the advice that is available to them?

I am myself a Canine Behaviourist, and the root cause of most of the problem cases I see is a failure to understand the dog's normal behaviour. There are without doubt bad dogs – temperamentally unsound, psychologically unstable, genetic throwbacks – but there are not as many of these as the euthanasia rate would seem to suggest. Nor indeed should the behaviour of the dog always be attributed to the fault of the owner. It is not true that "There are no bad dogs, only bad owners."

Why then do some dogs exhibit behaviour problems that seem on the face of it to be incurable?

There are many reasons, as we shall see, and the information in the following pages should be taken into consideration before any decision is made about whether the owner is an idiot or the dog is a rogue.

The book is divided into three parts. Part I explains how and why dogs act in the way they do. Part II deals with the most common causes of what we all see as problems in our dogs – and the ways in which I have found these problems can be made to disappear. Part III is an easy reference guide for those owners and trainers who have problem pets.

As an owner, a trainer, a competitor and a judge, I know the joy and frustration of handling problem pets. I also know that their problems can be solved, so long as we are prepared to understand how they learn to behave the way they do.

It is only through understanding how they learn that we shall be able to train them to obey our commands, which as you will see is very different to teaching them our values. To enable us to do this properly, we need to look at life with us humans from the dog's point of view. In other words, we need to *Think Dog*!

Part I
What Is a Dog?

1   Where Dogs Come From

My appointments diary read: Monday, 9 a.m. – Miss Gort with two-year-old male Rottweiler – aggressive to people. "What a wonderful start to a fresh week," I remember thinking as I heard her car pull into our shingle car park. Little did I know just how important this case was going to be in proving that the key to solving problem behaviour in dogs lies in establishing the root cause and not just trying to control the symptom.

When I went out to meet her, I was met by the sight of a frail lady in her late sixties, clutching the handle of the car's tail-gate, desperately trying to keep her footing. The reason why she was having so much trouble was because, in her other hand, straining furiously on the end of a lead was a huge, extremely angry-looking Rottweiler. To make matters worse, his anger was definitely directed towards me. My further thoughts were a mixture of: "Will she be able to hang on to it?" and "Why does a woman of her age choose to own a dog of this size?"

She did manage to hang on and, to cut a long story short, she did not choose the dog, she inherited it. Miss Gort used to be the housekeeper for a retired Army officer. Rudi, as the dog was called, was originally owned by him. He died and left instructions in his will that Miss Gort should have the house and the dog. An adequate amount of money was also left to make sure that his instructions that Rudi should have the best of everything would not prove to be a hardship.

Within a short space of time, Rudi had become unmanageable and Miss Gort thought he probably needed training. It became abundantly clear, when Rudi dragged her off the seat that she was perched on and dumped her straight onto the floor of my office, just because I left my chair to make us both a cup of tea, that Rudi was not in a trainable frame of mind.

Luckily, Miss Gort managed to hold on to his lead because I am certain that Rudi had not rushed forward to help me carry the cups.

We had a situation where, since the death of his master, Rudi was the only adult male in the house. Because of his sheer strength and size, Miss Gort found it impossible to exercise him to the extent that he needed. On top of this, she was following her former employer's wishes to the letter and Rudi was being fed three times a day on a variety of fresh butcher's mince, hearts, liver, etc.

Before anything could be done about Rudi, he had to be brought under control. This involved a combination of restricting his access around the house and denying him certain privileges that he had come to accept as rights; changing his diet to one that was well balanced and designed to take the "fizz" out of him quickly; and using some of the money to employ an experienced dog walker who would be able to give Rudi regular "off territory exercise" and more mental stimulation. This last piece of advice was also designed to reduce his very pronounced territorial attitude and, in my opinion, was a better way of spending the money – so that Rudi could have the best – than running up a large weekly butcher's bill. (All of these techniques will be discussed in detail later.)

This simple combination produced remarkable results within a short space of time and Rudi turned out to be a very nice, gentle giant – as are the vast majority of this breed. Had we attempted a training approach to cure the problem whilst Rudi was in this under-exercised, under-stimulated, over-dominant and diet-related over-excitable state, we would definitely have failed. The chances are that we would probably have got quite badly bitten in the process.

I received a Christmas card from Miss Gort that year and, inside it was a photograph of Rudi standing up at the kitchen sink, apparently doing the washing up. I think it was meant to show that she had eventually tamed her man.

What was wrong with him was not that he was aggressive, just that he was acting in an aggressive manner and I hope that what follows will show you that there is a difference – I actually like Rottweilers and I do not think that they deserve the bad press that they receive. Amongst the other contributory factors, Rudi had been given the role of leader in the "human/canine pack" within that household, and was living up to what he saw as his responsibilities.

At first it may seem bizarre to talk of a household as a pack.

We humans do not see it that way, but that is how it seems to the dog, because as we shall see, dogs are by nature bound to be members of a pack. They are born that way.

ANCESTRY

To understand the behaviour of dogs it is necessary to look at the behaviour of the species from which they have descended. By studying the blueprint, we can start to form a clearer picture of *why* dogs behave in the way they do. Of course, when you consider the difference in size between, for instance a Great Dane and a Chihuahua, it seems difficult to accept that both of these breeds originated from one standard blueprint. Yet there is reliable evidence that the dog is descended mainly from a single species, active in Northern Europe more than ten thousand years ago. This does not rule out the possibility that in other regions the dog as we know it was also evolving from nomadic relatives of this same species.

Even though the dimensions of the modern domestic dog differ from breed to breed, in 1937 E. Dahr found that the ratio of snout length to the width of the upper jaw at its narrowest point was, on average, constant in all dogs and that it was the same as the ratios of the skull dimensions of Stone Age dogs. He then compared the length of the row of molar teeth to the height of the lower jaw and obtained similar results. It would seem from these studies that when dogs were first being domesticated their skulls were all of similar dimensions and therefore evolved from the same type.

This conclusion is also supported by the fact that all breeds of domestic dog have brain cases of approximately the same size. Therefore the difference between Chihuahua and Great Dane is purely one of size and shape of body – and it is man made.

If all dogs have evolved from the same species, what we need to establish is which species we should be examining. Is it (as most scientists believe) the wolf, or is it the jackal? We need to look at both species and form a conclusion based on species similarities, and on this basis the wolf becomes the most likely candidate as the forefather of the dog. First of all, the dental characteristics of the dog and the wolf are similar, whereas the arrangement of the jackal's teeth is different from both. Significantly, when in 1965 Scott and Fuller investigated ninety behaviour patterns in the domestic dog, they found that all but nineteen of them were present in the wolf. The vocal patterns of both the dog and the wolf are also similar, whilst the jackal's pattern again is distinctly different. So too is its social behaviour.

Based on the evidence available therefore, it would seem likely that the animal that we should be looking at is the wolf.

THE WAY OF THE WOLF

The wolf is a pack animal that lives within a very strong social structure where there is an established hierarchy. The Alpha wolf leads the pack. Contrary to popular opinion, he does not maintain that role by regularly showing aggression to the rest of the pack. His position of authority is upheld by constant displays of deference being shown to him by the rest of the members. For sure, if there is an up-and-coming dominant figure within the group who feels like challenging the leader's authority, then real aggression will become the order of the day, but these challenges are rare. In general the whole pack lives in harmony, and the human race can learn a lot from the way wolves band together to survive. Research has shown that feral dogs live in much the same way and exhibit remarkably similar behaviour.

For instance, when a female wolf has cubs, then quite often one or two other females in the pack will produce milk in case the natural mother gets killed. So too, what we call phantom pregnancies are quite common in the domestic dog and I recently heard of a case where a female Dobermann started to produce milk when the next door neighbour's cat had kittens – a rare occurrence I admit, but one that shows how strong a dog's maternal instincts are.

Wolves are very territorial: in order to survive, each pack must stake and defend its territory by defecating or urinating at strategic boundary points. Similar territory-marking behaviour can be seen on a daily basis from the domestic dog, even though its food is so easily available that in general the need to defend is not so great. Because we dictate that our dogs have to share exercise areas or because we insist that they have to be socialised, normally we do not have too many problems with territory guarding. However, if two very dominant dogs meet that have been regularly allowed by their owners to mark a particular territory, then all hell is going to break loose, especially if either or both of the dogs are hungry at the time.

The body posture of wolves and dogs is almost identical. We as humans can read the obvious signals in our dogs that portray fear, aggression, pleasure, submission etc., but we are incapable of reading the more subtle signs that are transmitted dog to dog. We tend to place our own interpretations on what our dog is trying to say.

To most people, the happy low tail wag of the Golden Retriever is the same as the high tail carriage and tip of tail wagging of the German Shepherd. The confusion is brought about by the variation of dog breeds that we meet on a daily basis. We might live with a Golden Retriever, who shows a low tail wag whenever we look at it, and then wonder why the German Shepherd, who carried his tail high and appeared to look happy, bit us when we went to stroke him.

If we lived with the blueprint, we would soon learn that the first is a submissive posture which says "I am no threat; please be gentle," whilst the other is a clear threat which says, "Come any closer and I will bite you." It is still more difficult to read a dog that has had its tail chopped off to comply with a breed standard!

Because the modern dog is on the whole a selectively bred animal, over the years breeders have pounced on what they have seen as desirable traits, and in some cases abnormalities, and propagated them – probably the reason why dogs exhibit some behaviour patterns not seen in the wolf. In the wild and left to nature, perhaps some of these man-made animals would not have survived; the survival of the fittest is very cruel but it is also very efficient at ensuring that only the best specimens are left to breed. It is a fact though, no matter how much we try to genetically engineer breed characteristic, size and shape, the way of the wolf will always remain as an unalterable instinct.

2   How a Dog's Mind Develops

All species of animal life go through predictable periods of development. In some species, including dogs, the onset of some of these periods, or phases, are predictable almost to the day. An awareness of the critical periods of development in the dog can help us to a greater understanding of its behaviour. For instance, all too frequently I see dogs with behavioural problems, the root cause of which has been ignorance on the part of the breeder. Dogs that have been bred for show purposes and "run on" to see if they make the grade, can suffer from a condition known as Kennelosis or Kennel Syndrome if they are kept in kennels up to and over the age of fourteen weeks. These dogs, if sold later as pets, often turn out to be the type of pets we would rather not have. They are unable to handle stressful situations and cannot really identify with people. Other dogs are their great love in life simply because they have missed out on the vitally important *Human Socialisation Period*. They have over-socialised with dogs and under-socialised with people.

Conversely, breeders who run puppy farms and the like, often take the puppies away from the mother far too soon, in some cases at four or five weeks old. Hundreds of them are then transported in very stressful conditions up and down the motorways to pick-up points where they are passed on to dealers, or delivered to kennels and pet shops which do a roaring trade in puppy sales. The unsuspecting buyer who purchases one of these cute balls of fluff learns to regret it when it grows up, simply because the puppy has never learnt how to be a dog. The critical period that they have missed out on is the *Canine Socialisation Period*. They often grow up to be dog aggressive, because they have never learned how to interact with other dogs, and they are usually difficult to train, because their mother was not around to discipline them during the first few formative weeks.

These two critical periods of development are vitally important in terms of how the dog will develop temperamentally. Far too many people attribute canine problem behaviour to inherited temperament, the inference being that nothing can be done about it because it has been passed on through the genes of either the mother or the father. In most cases, this is rubbish. To announce to the worried dog owner that the behaviour that is causing concern is inherited is a wonderful "cop out" for the person who has been asked, "Can you help me to cure my dog's behaviour?" and does not know how to.

Obviously, there are occasions when the behaviour is a direct result of genetic influence, but with most of the cases that I see the behaviour exhibited can be explained by some environmental circumstance and therefore will not have been passed on through the genes. The behaviour of a bitch can be passed on to her puppies on a "monkey see, monkey do" basis. For instance, a bitch that is very dominant within the household in which she lives may growl at everyone who comes to see her puppies. The pups will often copy her, and this behaviour could easily be attributed to a genetically inherited trait. Yet if you were to lower the rank of the bitch within the mixed human/canine pack, she would not growl at people that *you* let in, and the puppies would copy the deference that she showed towards *your* superior decision. It is important to note that puppies develop at an incredible rate between the ages of four to seven weeks, so much so, that by the time they are seven weeks old, they are transmitting adult brain waves and are therefore capable of learning by example.

Although environmental influence is only just beginning to be widely accepted in this country as a very real cause of some behaviour problems, critical periods of development were recognised many years ago. In 1963, Clarence Pfaffenberger wrote a book called *The New Knowledge of Dog Behaviour*. In his introduction Pfaffenberger wrote: "The dog family, to me, is the most interesting family in all animal life outside the family of man himself. In many ways he is much like man, so much so that we can sometimes study our own behaviour best by studying the behaviour of dogs, especially puppies.

"This is true because a dog's behaviour towards his human family (owners) is so much like that of a child towards his own family. A puppy's behaviour towards his own mother, and her behaviour towards him, are very similar to the child's behaviour towards his mother and the human mother's behaviour towards the child."

Primarily, *The New Knowledge of Dog Behaviour* is a story of how Pfaffenberger was assigned the task of finding the ideal puppy to become the ideal guide dog. However, the research he directed during the late 1950s was of far wider importance, as it identified the following critical periods of development common to all dogs.

NEONATAL (0 TO 13 DAYS)

It is during this period, as their senses develop, that puppies start to learn how to be dogs. At first, once they start to move around the whelping box, their behaviour is totally undog-like. During this period they are using their newly developing senses to explore the environment, and it is through a process of positive and negative reinforcement that they eventually learn to act, and be recognised, as dogs. They may, for example, explore the sides of the whelping box and then try to climb up it like a cat. When they end up flat on their backs on the floor, they learn, through this negative experience, that they cannot climb like cats. However, walking on all fours around the sides of the whelping box, they will bump into a litter mate and perhaps engage for the first time in what will eventually become play behaviour, or they may settle down with that litter mate to sleep. The positive experience that they receive from this ensures that in the future they will walk like a dog.

CANINE SOCIALISATION (14 TO 49 DAYS)

The more dog-like they become, the more do their rough and tumble games begin to have a definite purpose. Play fighting and biting with the needle-sharp teeth that Mother Nature gave them, teach them how hard to bite to cause pain, and by being bitten in return they learn what pain feels like. In fact, the only purpose that these needle-sharp teeth have *is* to cause pain.

At this stage in their life, their teeth are of no use for tearing meat, chewing bones, hunting or any other adult dog activity. Puppies have very weak, under-developed jaw muscles and it is during this period that they must learn how to regulate their strength of bite. By biting the ear of a litter mate, they cause a yelp, and they then know that they have bitten too hard. The nip that they get in return teaches them just what biting too hard feels like.

As this period progresses, the mother usually starts to wean the puppies. (Some bitches are more maternal than others and therefore this is variable.) She gives a low warning growl and if a puppy does not immediately respond, then she disciplines it by snarling at the puppy and making piercing eye contact. She may even stand over the puppy, who, by this time, is usually squealing and lying flat on its back. The next time she gives the warning growl that puppy will respond immediately.

This is one of the ways that the puppy learns the meaning of discipline during the canine socialisation period. Unfortunately, some breeders who witness a mother exhibiting this sort of behaviour, especially towards one of the puppies she recognises as being a particularly dominant character, often take the view that the mother does not like that puppy and might well kill it. As a result, they often separate the mother from that puppy or take the puppy away from the litter and hand rear it. It is very rare indeed for a mother to kill a puppy at this stage in its development. It is, however, extremely important that the puppies stay with their litter brothers, sisters and mother throughout this period, if they are to grow up to be well-balanced individuals. By not allowing the mother to discipline a dominant character properly, the breeder is passing on a whole bundle of trouble to any future owners of that dog.

Although the main function of this canine socialisation period is to enable the puppy to learn how to regulate its strength of bite, how to socialise with other dogs and how to establish pecking orders, it is also vitally important that it experiences human contact.

Breeders should handle each and every puppy on a regular basis, pick them up, gently turn them over, check the ears, eyes, teeth, feet etc. By doing this, not only are they teaching the puppies that human contact is a pleasurable experience, they are also subjecting these puppies to minute amounts of stress, which will help to build up the body's stress reserve levels for later life. Puppies who have been allowed to complete this period with the warmth, security and companionship of the mother and litter mates, together with the contact that they should experience from people, generally grow up to be well-adjusted adult dogs.

HUMAN SOCIALISATION (7 TO 12 WEEKS)

Having learnt how to be dogs during the first period of their development, the puppies should now learn now to be dogs within a human environment. The ideal age to take a puppy away from the litter is at seven weeks (49 days). At this age a good breeder should call on the help of a knowledgeable trainer or behaviourist to carry out aptitude tests on each and every one of the litter.

A series of non-stressful tests can be completed at this age, which will give an indication of the likely temperament and character of each puppy when it grows up, enabling the breeder to match the puppy to the family to which he or she intends to send it. What is being tested is the puppies' genetic potential which will differ from dog to dog. If tested later the effects of the environment will probably influence the results. The role of the breeder here can be crucial. I have lost count of the number of owners who have told me that they did not choose their dog, it chose them. When they arrived to look at all the pups, theirs just pushed the others out of the way and threw itself at them. If the prospective owners asked the breeder, they would usually be told that this pup was the first to the food bowl and had grown bigger and stronger than the others because, right from when it was born, it always rooted out and suckled from the bitch's most lucrative inguinal teat (the pendulous most productive teat in the groin area). The breeder would already have recognised this pup as the most dominant and boldest in the litter.

This choice of ownership, having been made by the dog and not the human, is normally just the first of many other decisions that the dog will make instead of the other way around.

Most of us know that it is not a good idea to decide to take the cringing smallest puppy that hides in the corner of the room and is ignored by its litter mates, although many people let their hearts rule their heads and take that one home out of pity. But not many people can foresee the problems that may arise by taking home "the one that chose them". If all that you are looking for is a well mannered and easily manageable family pet, then you should choose the fairly confident, but not too pushy, puppy.

In an ideal world, the breeder should decide, firstly, if you are the type of owner that he/she wants one of the puppies to go to and secondly, having assessed exactly your type of domestic environment, decide which of the pups would be best suited to that environment. Unfortunately, we do not live in an ideal world, and too many breeders are "in it" only for financial gain.

Over the years, various tests have been designed to evaluate puppies for specific types of work. Pfaffenberger developed tests to select those puppies most likely to become responsible guide dogs. In 1975 William E. Campbell devised tests to select those most likely to be good family pets, and it is these tests that should be of interest to all breeders who want to sell puppies as pets.

It goes without saying that they should be conducted by someone who knows what he/she is doing and who, ideally, is a stranger to the pups. The test area should be a room that is unfamiliar to the pups and the test time should be when the pups are at their most active. Each puppy is tested individually in order to ensure that the results are not influenced by the extra confidence that might be given by the presence of the rest of its litter mates.

There are five separate areas of behaviour to be tested, and on each one the tester will mark the puppy as follows:

Very dominant	Score 1
Dominant	Score 2
Submissive	Score 3
Very submissive	Score 4
Independent	Score 5

Dogs that score mainly ones would probably be suited to guard dog/police dog work, provided the handler is experienced and the dog is physically capable of this type of work (I suppose a very dominant Chihuahua would have to become an undercover police dog). On no account should this type of dog be sold as a pet to an inexperienced person. A mixture of ones and twos, but mainly twos would still make a good working dog.

Those that score twos and threes, but mainly twos, could be classified as pets, but again preferably for experienced owners and those with older or no children. Mainly threes would be good pets with younger children around.

Threes and fours would need to go to a very sensitive and

calm environment. The dog that scores a lot of fours could easily become a fear biter.

Dogs that score mainly fives would probably handle a kennel environment quite well, but would not necessarily be a rewarding pet.

The tests should be conducted in the following way:-

1. *Social attraction*

The pup should be placed on the floor in the middle of the test area and the tester should attract its attention and encourage it to approach in a direction away from where it entered.

The readiness to approach, the manner and body postures it displays as it approaches and its attitude to the tester should all be taken into account. Coming readily, tail up, jumping up and gnawing the tester's hands would score 1. Coming very hesitantly, tail tucked in, possibly submissively urinating would score 4. Totally ignoring the tester and doing its own thing would obviously score 5.

2. *Following*

Having stroked the pup for coming, or going to it and stroking it if it did not come, the tester should walk away and observe how readily the puppy follows. The very dominant pup would follow readily, probably keep getting underfoot and might even attempt to bite the feet. The very submissive would have to be coaxed gently and would probably follow in fits and starts, rolling on to its back each time the tester stopped or bent down to stroke it. Score 5 would still be doing its own thing.

3. *Restraint*

The tester would gently roll the puppy on to its back and hold it there for approximately thirty seconds. The grading, which here can only be between 1 and 4, would depend upon whether it struggled fiercely and tried to bite, just struggled but did not bite, struggled but eventually settled or offered no resistance and licked the tester's hand.

4. *Social dominance*

The head, neck and shoulder regions on a dog are dominant areas. Watch two high ranking dogs meeting and quite often you will see a paw or the chin of the slightly higher ranking dog being placed across the withers of the other. By crouching down, the tester can stroke the puppy quite firmly from the head down over the withers, and continue to do this for thirty seconds. If the pup scored 1, it is because it objected, possibly growled and tried to reverse this domination by jumping up. Score 4 probably collapsed in a heap and squirted more urine. Score 5 just walked off and totally ignored the whole proceedings.

5. *Elevation dominance*

By bending over and forming a cradle with the hands under the belly of the pup, the tester gently lifts the pup a few inches off the floor and holds it in that position for about thirty seconds. This puts the tester into a position of total control and the pup into a position of having absolutely no control at all. The manner in which the pup accepts, or otherwise, will determine the score of 1 to 4. As in test three (Restraint) a score of 5 cannot be recorded because the puppy is not in a position to display an independent attitude.

At seven weeks of age, except for a small amount of learned behaviour, the puppies are almost clean slates. The way in which they respond will show their true genetic potential. Later on, the environment in which they will be raised will have some impact on their temperaments when they reach adulthood, but by assessing them at this age, the breeder can ensure that, as far as possible, the right pup goes to the right family.

Once the pup is in its new family, it is important that all contact with humans, including strangers, visitors, etc., should be pleasurable experiences. The new owners should avoid reprimanding the dog as far as possible and should take great pains to avoid physical punishment of any kind. The eight to eleven week period is also known as the Fear-Imprint Period. If, at this time, the puppy experiences trauma or fright, the result may well be that the the circumstances leading up to that fright will become so deep-rooted that it will be difficult to eradicate it later on. The new owner should be particularly aware of this period in its development and wherever possible try to avoid traumatic experiences. The first visit to the veterinary surgeon may well be during this time and it is as well, and well worth the expense, to make an appointment to see the vet simply to have him or her fondle the puppy, give it the occasional titbit and allow it to go home again.

SENIORITY CLASSIFICATION PERIOD (12 TO 16 WEEKS)

It is around this age that puppies begin to change into young adults. They begin to grow in confidence within their familiar environment: they begin to take liberties and are sometimes granted privileges which, if they were still with their mother and litter brothers and sisters, or if they were in a feral dog or wolf pack, would not be allowed. We, as humans, still regard the twelve- to sixteen-week old dog as a puppy, and are, therefore, more tolerant towards some of the things that it does that we would not tolerate from an adult dog. We must, however, be aware that puppies and dogs develop at a greater rate than humans, and just as we would not accept cheekiness from a ten- or twelve-year-old child, we should not accept the cheeky behaviour of the twelve- to sixteen-week-old puppy.

This period is also known as the Age of Cutting: cutting new teeth, and cutting mother's apron strings. In other words the puppies are becoming much more confident in their own ability and are trying, for the first time, to establish some sort of rank within the canine/human pack in which they live.

Over the past few years, Dr Ian Dunbar has been conducting research in California on how dog/dog socialisation and dog/human socialisation during the period twelve to eighteen weeks can have a long-term beneficial effect on the behaviour in the adult dog. This socialisation involves puppy kindergarten classes, where little dogs learn not to be frightened of big dogs and big dogs know how to conduct themselves around little dogs. During the sessions, the organisers prepare the young dogs for the sort of things that they will experience in later life, such as medical checks on their toenails, ears, eyes, nose, anal glands, etc. The whole family, including children, are encouraged to attend these classes, and the children are taught how to teach their young dogs how to come when called, stay, heel etc.

At the same time the young dogs learn that the companionship of erratic, quick-moving children, who have high-pitched voices and are not unpredictable in what they will do is a pleasurable experience and not something about which to be frightened or, more importantly, defensive.

The period of twelve to eighteen weeks was chosen for the following reasons:
1. Twelve weeks is about the earliest that veterinary surgeons

will allow the owners to let their puppies mix with other dogs, because of the vaccinations that all young puppies should receive.

2. Eighteen weeks in a dog's development is a time when tremendous changes take place. In the males the testosterone level starts to rise, and their attitudes start to change, not only theirs towards other dogs but also other dogs towards them. In a nutshell, they are no longer puppies.

These puppy kindergarten classes are beginning to be introduced in this country and I would advise all new dog owners with young puppies to seek veterinary advice on where the nearest one is to them. The research results are conclusive. Puppies who have attended puppy kindergarten classes do grow up to be better dogs. They rarely get involved in dog fights. They rarely show aggression to owners or other humans, and veterinary surgeons find them much easier to treat as patients.

FLIGHT INSTINCT PERIOD (4 TO 8 MONTHS)

Flight instinct could also be described as the call of the wild. It is a time when the young dog, who has responded quite readily and happily to being recalled in the past, suddenly stands still with a faraway look in its eye and then decides to go in the opposite direction.

In the wild this would be perfectly normal behaviour. The young dog/bitch would, perhaps, set out looking for a responsive female/male (around this time most females come into season for the first time), or just explore territory on its own. The equivalent in the human would be age fourteen to sixteen years old.

Flight instinct does not cover the whole period of four to eight months, it is usually just a few days to perhaps a month, at some time within that period. Future deep-rooted recall problems can depend on just how much fun the young dog experiences from his response to the call of the wild. If, having run off, a young male dog, for example, puts up a rabbit and gives chase; on route, he finds a family has just left their picnic to play ball in the park and he is able to eat their cakes, sandwiches and ice-cream; having just finished that, he meets a pretty little bitch who engages upon a good romp around the park – and then after a period of about two hours he suddenly comes across his owner who, from the dog's point of view, has blue sparks coming out of his ears, there would be no competition. Going back to the owner is bad news, running off would appear to be good news.

Dog owners should be aware of this natural instinct and pay particular attention to their dogs throughout this period. The moment they get the feeling that the dog has an urge to wanderlust on a familiar exercise area, the dog should be exercised on a long leash or flexileash. Alternatively, exercise off leash can be conducted in areas not known to the dog. Exercising off familiar territory tends to have the effect of the pack sticking together much more closely, provided, of course, as is explained in Chapter 3, the dog recognises the owner as the leader of the pack.

ONSET OF PUBERTY – (6 TO 14 MONTHS)

During this period certain hormonal changes come over both dogs and bitches. The body's ability to handle changes in hormones is relevant to the dog in the same way as the same problem is relevant to the young adult human.

Some young people develop spots, some develop irrational attitude problems, some just breeze through it with no problems at all (but not many). Those of us who are parents know how traumatic this hormone surge can be for our children. We also know how worrying and frustrating it is for us.

The onset of puberty takes its toll on dogs in much the same way: whilst the body is struggling to handle the new hormone surge, side effects start to come to the fore. Slight changes in behaviour become evident, one of which could be fear of familiar situations. The classic example would be that the dog comes across something that it has seen on, perhaps, a daily basis for many months but suddenly does not seem to recognise as a familiar object. It may bark, growl and back away from that object. How the dog's owner handles the situation can determine part of the dog's character for the rest of its life. If, for example, the dog started to bark at a familiar chair which had been put in a slightly different place and the owner tried to reassure the dog while encouraging it to approach the chair, then for the rest of the dog's life it may remain frightened of that chair, the reason being that encouragement had been construed as rewarding behaviour ("There's a good boy").

If, however, the owner recognised this as a "fear of familiar situation" problem, he would say, "Don't be such a stupid dog," then would sit in the chair and ignore the dog until the dog approached. Normally, the act of sitting in the chair would encourage the dog to approach immediately, with the attitude, "Oh! It's *that* chair. I didn't recognise it out of its place."

How you handle irrational behaviour can form a pattern as to how the dog behaves in the future. Initially, we should be aware of the effects of puberty in young dogs and young adult humans and we should take the view that we would not reward abnormal behaviour by trying to reassure, comfort, praise etc. By the same token, we cannot punish irrational behaviour, because there is no logic behind it.

We can, however, make sure by our off-hand reaction that the behaviour is not going to be rewarded. If there is no improvement over the next few days, then we can start to look for some other reason, but initially awareness of this period in the puppy's development is sufficient.

MATURITY (1 TO 4 YEARS)

Up to the age of approximately four months, the critical periods of development are very much the same for every breed of dog. Following that, there are slight variations. In general, small dogs enter each individual phase before larger dogs. The onset of full maturity spreads between one to four years depending on the breed and size of the dog.

The onset of full maturity heralds the onset of a second seniority classification period. During this time the dog will try to stamp its identity within the pack situation once and for all. (Readers with adult dogs where this has happened need not despair. Chapters 3, 5 and 6 will show that a rearrangement of the pecking order is quite possible without confrontation.) During this period, if the dog has been able to attain a high rank during the first seniority classification period (twelve to sixteen weeks), then, depending upon the temperament of the dog, any challenge for pack leadership between dog and human may become aggressive. Whether this will happen or not depends on the type of dog with which we are dealing, and on what the owner does.

Some dogs have what is known as active defence reflexes.

Some dogs have passive defence reflexes. A dog with active defence reflexes, when challenged, will meet that challenge with aggression. A dog with passive defence reflexes, when challenged, will meet that challenge with a display of total submission or alternatively with hyperactive or stupid puppy behaviour (see Chapter 14).

If you have allowed your dog, especially one of the guarding breeds, to attain a high rank within your human/dog pack and you decide to challenge that dog over a particular issue, then it is quite likely that you will encourage an aggressive confrontation. The Alpha-figure in a wolf pack would discipline all lower-ranking members that tried to take privileges which they did not deserve. This does not make the dog an aggressive dog, it merely makes it a high-ranking dog acting in an aggressive manner. The way that your dog reacts when it reaches full maturity is, basically, a culmination of what it has been allowed to get away with during the critical periods of development leading up to this time. The inclusion of a chapter on the critical periods of development is designed to enable new dog owners to make sure that, when their dog reaches full maturity, they reach it with a clear insight into their role within the pack situation. For readers with dogs who are already mature and are exhibiting behaviour problems which involve aggression, the following chapters should be of help.

3   The Dog in the Human Pack

As we have seen from the foregoing chapters, all dogs, regardless of their size or shape, still display the same behaviour patterns as their distant ancestors, and they all go through the same periods of development. Over the years, however, we have succeeded in altering the basic design to a point, where, in some cases, it has become unrecognisable from the original blueprint. It is because we have achieved such a wide variety of breeds to meet the needs and fancies of different people that the dog has become so popular. It has almost become the standard idea that the average family is incomplete until it has a house, a car, 2.5 children and a dog. Yet, if more people realised that the cute little poodle, fast asleep on the warm lap of some doting owner, has all the instincts of a wild animal, then they might not so readily accept the dog into their family as an equal.

Over the centuries the domestication of dogs has resulted in their being, generally, subservient to man. Despite this fact, as can be seen from the last chapter, unless the dog is socialised with humans before it is fourteen weeks of age, the chances of forming a strong bond with it is pretty slim, and some would say impossible. Therefore, it is obvious that any empathy we have with the dog is not hereditary. It is imprinted from an early age. This early socialisation and the fact that we are upright creatures, which gives us the appearance of being the more dominant animal, help us to maintain our control over dogs. Occasionally, we lose that control and we end up with dogs that bite the hand that feeds them.

If we can forget for a while the various breed differences, and look upon the dog as a creature with inherited instincts, it soon becomes obvious why these circumstances arise. Whether we are considering the social structure of wolves, feral dogs or the domestic dog, we are looking at a pack animal. For the social structure to hold together every pack needs an Alpha (leader) figure. Understanding the rules in a wolf/feral dog pack is relatively easy for the members of those packs because they have an established pecking order, wherein every individual knows its place. The higher ranking they are within their society, the more privileges they are granted. They all display and are capable of reading the same body postures and signals. If a lower-ranking individual tries to take a privilege that would normally be reserved for the Alpha figure, invariably a withering look from the Alpha is all that is required to ensure that order is maintained. When we look at the domestic dog we can see that, by virtue of the fact that they live within a mixed species pack, understanding the rules becomes confusing. We, as humans, attempt to teach the dog our values. The dog is only capable of learning on a canine level and can only understand canine values. In general, we muddle by and it is a tribute to the dog that it eventually learns to live with such inconsistent creatures as ourselves.

If we take a look at some of the rights and privileges that are afforded to the Alpha figure and compare them with the way that some of us live with our dogs, we can start to see where the communication between the species starts to break down and how we can end up with what we term as a problem or disobedient dog.

Many of my clients tell me that their dog is allowed to jump up next to them on the settee or chair whilst they are watching the television. The majority of these dogs are also allowed on to the bed, if only for a cuddle in the morning. Almost all of these dogs have their own baskets or bean-bags to sleep on. Many of them also like to occupy another area in the house as a favourite resting-place, under the kitchen table or behind a chair in the lounge, etc. When I ask my clients if these places are comfortable, they tell me that they assume so but that they have never tried them.

It is the right of the Alpha figure to sleep where it wishes but nobody sleeps in its bed.

In these households, however, it is the dog's bedspace that is inviolate, while it can sleep where it likes. Who is Alpha there?

Dogs are predators; therefore food is of prime importance to them, not just for survival, but as a means of maintaining the social order. Recently, a client of mine told me that her husband worked odd hours. Sometimes, because of his working arrangements, they ate their evening meal early, at 5 pm; sometimes they ate at 7 pm. The dog was always fed at 6 pm. What she could not understand was why, when they ate early, the dog never begged from the table, yet, when they ate later, he always begged, despite the fact he was never given food.

It is the right of the Alpha figure to have the richest pickings and obviously to eat first. The rest of the pack can have what is left unless the leader decides to have some some.

When the family ate first, even though the dog was obviously hungry, his instincts told him to wait for what was left of the pickings. However, when he was allowed to eat first, his instincts told he was also entitled to the food that was left, which the family were eating. (Possession comes into this area, see food-guarding in Chapter 13.)

One of the most popular games to play with any young dog is tug-of-war. In fact, there are tug toys available in pet shops designed to give both the human and the dog their own end to hold. We usually allow the dogs to win these games because we admire the tenacity and dedication that they put into them despite what we see as our superior strength. Similarly, rough and tumble games are great fun to play, until the youngster starts to get a bit aggressive, and then it is we who give up before it gets out of hand.

Being a predator and part of the hunting unit, the instinct not to get injured is much to the fore, and for this reason all dominant/submissive levels are decided through play.

We should not teach our young dogs that to growl, pull and persevere brings the reward of winning, and that when we engage upon a rough and tumble we then give up.

Many of my clients admit that, when they are going upstairs, their dog rushes in front of them and then turns on the top step and waits for them to come up towards them. We think nothing of it, and we usually glance down at the step in front. Look how this must appear to the dog.

On a daily basis, the rest of the pack shows deference towards the leader.

Canine or lupine displays of deference are exhibited by low head carriage coming towards and upwards, but avoiding any eye contact.

Doorways are a key area in the house as far as the dog is concerned. The doorway is the entrance to the den; it is also a narrow passageway. All too often I am told that the dog pushes past the owner through doorways. This is usually regarded as excitement on the part of the dog. Quite often too I am told how lazy the dog is: it spreads itself across the opening to the kitchen (or some other busy room in the house) and if told to move it just stretches and groans. Usually the owner ends up not disturbing the dog whilst it is sleeping but goes round the sleeping animal.

In the wild if the Alpha wants to walk across a clearing, all the other members of the pack move out of the way, not through fear but out of total respect.

If the Alpha is resting, all others make sure it is not disturbed. When approaching a narrow passageway, all others hang back to let the Alpha through first. All these are lupine/canine instincts. If you think about them, they are also human instincts. Rank has its privileges.

How many times have you been seated, intent upon a particular programme or news bulletin on the television, when suddenly your arm is forced in the air by your dog, wanting to be stroked? In most cases, we respond immediately, partly because we know that if we do not the dog will persevere and it will interrupt our viewing, and partly because we do not want the dog to think that it is unloved. Anyway, if the truth were known, we are flattered by the display of affection that the dog is showing us.

What is actually happening is the dog has decided who is going to stroke it, when and for how long it will be stroked. If you called your dog over to you during the evening, it is quite possible that you would get a look, a stretch and a groan but no other response. You would normally smile and take the view that you should "let sleeping dogs lie".

Without realising it we have a situation where from our dog's point of view:
1. It sleeps wherever it wants, but nobody sleeps in its bed.
2. It gets the pickings of available food and we have whatever is left.
3. It can win all fighting and strength games.
4. On a daily basis we show deference to its superior rank.
5. We allow it to precede us through narrow openings and we do not disturb it when we move around.
6. We respond to its demands for affection but we accept its refusal to comply with our demands.

All these are the rights of the Alpha figure. Our dogs do not ask for them; we grant them without realising it. If we inadvertently promote our dog to this high rank, we must accept the fact that the dog will take on the responsibility of the job that we have given it to do.

It is the responsibility of the Alpha to:

1. Lead the pack. That is why it pulls on the lead.
2. Keep the pack together. That is why it runs backwards and forwards when it is off the lead. If you take note, it is always running in a circle around us. It is herding us.
3. Protect the pack. That is why it is aggressive to other dogs that invade our territory or warns off joggers that do the same.
4. Initiate the hunt. That is usually what it is doing when we complain that it runs off.
5. Defend the den. That is why it is aggressive, or over-exuberant to visitors.

The list is endless and many other similar behaviour patterns will be discussed in later chapters. Dogs that exhibit them are not necessarily bad, disobedient or aggressive dogs; they are usually just dogs who are accepting the responsibilities with which we have unwittingly burdened them.

REVERSING THE ROLES

When looked upon in this light, it can be seen that if we assert ourselves as leaders of our pack, the majority of what we term as training problems will quickly disappear. We should:

1. Make sure that the dog does not sleep on our chairs or beds but we can sit in its place – it seems silly but it works.
2. Prepare the dog's food in its presence, then sit down to eat a sandwich or even a meal before we allow the dog to have its meal.
3. Make sure that all games are controlled by us – retrieving, hunt the titbit etc. – but refuse to enter into strength games.
4. Make sure that we occupy the top step so that the dog comes up to us, or deny it access to the upstairs area (the human den): fitting a baby gate is the easiest way of achieving this.
5. Slam a door in its face when it tries to push through the first crack of light that appears (be careful not to trap its nose) – it will quickly learn to take a pace back.

6. Make the dog move out of our way when we move about the house.

We should make the dog earn all of its privileges, stroking, eating, being let out etc. All demands should be met by an instruction to "Sit", "Down", or "Stay", just something simple to ensure that if the dog wants something from us he has to earn it first.

We should meet all attempts to mouth arms, hands or any part of the body, clothing or leash, with the loudest "Get off" combined with the most piercing eye contact that we can muster. No praise should be given when the dog stops.

These simple procedures are values that the canine mind can understand. They establish us as leaders and initiators of all activities and not the other way round. Above all, it is of prime importance that the rules of your pack are established before you leave your den. For instance, instinct dictates that dogs do not walk in front of a higher ranking individual and that the leader keeps the pack together. So if the dog is given the opportunity of pulling you to the park or refusing to come back when it is called, then you are allowing it to increase its status and you will lose the right to govern the terms of your relationship.

It is as well to point out that hundreds of dogs are being granted many privileges without it affecting their behaviour. The point I am making is that, if you have a dog that is exhibiting some sort of behaviour or control problem, then it is as well to look at the way you live with that dog to see whether, without realising it, you are granting it the privilege of a higher rank than yourself.

Rearranging the pecking order can be established by denying your dog the privileges reserved for the highest ranking. It is important though that this is done without physical confrontation. Imagine what would happen if a lower ranking wolf tried to challenge physically a higher ranking wolf.

In my practice, I have a way of demonstrating to the owners how to reduce their dogs' rank and the benefits that can be derived from it.

Normally, upon arrival the dog will pull the owner all the way from the car park to my office. I usually enquire whether they have attended formal training classes with the dog or not. Invariably the answer is that they have but they cannot stop it from pulling.

Once we have all settled into the office and teas and coffees have been supplied, I invite the owner to let the dog loose but to ignore all but the most obnoxious behaviour. My reasoning is that when a pack is on what is clearly someone else's territory, there is a slight amount of insecurity exhibited by the members of that pack. We can read the obvious human signs: sitting forward in seats; glances between a couple before anyone answers a question, even one as simple as "Would you like tea or coffee?"

Dogs, who rely on body signals to communicate, pick up on these signals plus many more too subtle for us to notice. If the pack is insecure, the leader should take charge and on these occasions, more often than not, the leader turns out to be the dog. It usually starts pacing backwards and forwards, always between me and the family. This sort of behaviour is usually described as the sort of hyperactive behaviour that the dog exhibits if it visits anyone, or they have visitors themselves. When, I am assured, they are on their own, it is usually quite calm. If the dog is ignored, i.e. not told to lie down, or stroked in an attempt to calm what is obviously restlessness, then it starts to display a variety of attention-seeking activities.

It will whine at the door in an attempt to be let out, it will bark at the slightest sound in an attempt to be told to shut up – it will not care whether the attention is good or bad. It will raid my wastepaper basket, climb on the furniture or attempt to get on the laps of the owners.

The way that the dog behaves tells me a lot about how it views its role within the pack. The questions I ask the owners about the privileges that it is allowed at home usually confirm what I am seeing. Because I also ignore the dog up to this point, the dog gets the impression that I am also lower ranking than it. Having explained to the owners exactly what has been happening whilst we have been chatting, I tell them that I am going to establish the right to lead in my den and on my territory, and explain the essential criteria:

1. A lower ranking dog would not normally approach a higher ranking dog with a view to taking a bone away from it. It would look from a respectful distance, and if the higher ranking dog was not prepared to give up that bone, piercing eye contact would result in the lower ranking dog averting its gaze immediately.

2. A lower ranking dog would not normally precede a higher ranking dog through a narrow opening. Watch a pack of Fox

Hounds being released from their kennels, and you will see that the same dog comes out first on every occasion.

3. A lower ranking dog would not approach a higher ranking dog and put its paws or teeth on that dog as a form of greeting. It would approach only with the right amount of deference that the ranking animal allowed.

Dogs who have undergone the right amount of canine socialisation already know that these are basic canine manners. I take the view that all dogs are trained how to be dogs at seven weeks of age; we humans then take them into our pack and confuse them. All I need to do is remind them of their early lessons.

At this point, I would add that I do not use the following technique on dogs that are potentially aggressive towards people – I establish the same rules with these dogs but I use the techniques described in Chapter 6.

I take a titbit and hold it between my finger and thumb. I do not offer it or look at the dog. I continue to speak to the owners. Usually the dog goes through its learned repertoire of tricks: it sits, it gives a paw, it might even bark. Once it realises that none of these things is bringing the expected reward, it just climbs up to take it. I say gently "Get off"; if it does not immediately remove its mouth I roar "GET OFF", and at the same time make piercing eye contact. All dogs were taught by their mothers when they were being weaned that "Get off the milk bar" meant get off immediately or suffer mum's wrath. I do not reward the dog for getting off. It was my food and I do not want the dog to take it. I put the titbit away and after a minute I move about the office and call the dog over to me, praising it for responding to my call.

A little later I pick up the titbit. If the dog has not learned I say gently "Get off". Very rarely do I have to back it up, as most dogs immediately remove their mouths and avert eye contact. Rule one is established – *Do not take my bone!*

Next I go to the door and encourage the dog to follow me. I want to teach him not to push past me. My office is a converted stable, so the door opens outwards. Without saying anything to the dog, I start to open the door. As soon as the first crack of light appears, out of habit the dog dashes for it. Before his nose gets into the crack, I slam the door. Again without saying anything, I repeat the procedure. On the fourth or fifth occasion, as I push the door open, the dog steps back. I walk through and close the door behind me. The reason I have said nothing is because I do not want the dog to perform a trick. I want him to afford me the privilege of going first without me having to ask.

Rule two is established – *I go through narrow openings first.*

At this point I stay out of the office for a few minutes. When I return I want to be able to go in and greet the dog without having my hand grasped in his jaw, however gently, or his paws all over me. These may be social gestures, but they are also very dominant forms of canine greeting behaviour. I show friendship by stroking the dog's head, neck and shoulder regions (socially significant areas), but any attempt to dominate me in turn will be met by a gentle "Get off" accelerated as required, but rarely necessary. Most dogs are, by this time, keyed in to this quiet warning that they are overstepping their rank. When I run my hands over the withers I am looking for a subtle acceptance of any pressure I care to exert. Usually during our initial greeting I feel resistance to pressure, however slight it may be.

This subtle resistance or acceptance is surely what dog to dog greeting is all about, but something which the human eye never perceives, and would explain why when one dog puts a paw or chin across the withers of another, sometimes there is a fight and sometimes not.

Rule three is established – *Greeting behaviour is on my terms!*

Having reminded the dog what canine manners are and assuming I feel an acceptance of any pressure I care to exert on the withers, I know that the dog will not pull me on the lead because a stare and a growl will ensure that it does not walk in front of me. It will come to me if I show friendship. It will stop barking, growling and jumping on anyone entering my den if I so wish, because my rank is such that I have the right to govern all movements at the entrance to my den. This demonstration does not give the owners any greater control over their dog, all that it does is enable them to see what benefits they will get from attaining a higher rank. Establishing yourself as pack leader is not a new concept when it comes to training dogs. Using canine psychology instead of the old "push and pull" training methods is.

I think it will, by now, have become quite clear how akin the social structure of the canine species is to the human species. We observe exactly the same code of conduct towards higher ranking people as dogs do towards higher ranking dogs. Accepting the fact that the mutual benefits of feeding, hunting, guarding etc., brought us together in the first place, I am convinced that what has kept us together for countless generations is our similarities in basic manners and recognition of rank. In fact, because we observe the same instinctive rules, man and dog could be regarded as soul mates. Our modern way of life is actually granting our dogs privileges that we would only grant to higher ranking humans and this is an area that we need to consider.

What will give you the right and the rank to lead your dog is: understanding your dog's ancestry and accepting that most of its behaviour is instinctive and therefore needs guiding, not suppressing; being aware of what is happening to it as it progresses through the critical periods of development; ensuring that you do not grant it privileges to the point where it gets a false idea about its role within your pack; and establishing the same code of conduct that its mother established at the earliest possible stage in its life. To re-establish that code of conduct requires that you first understand what affects the way dogs learn.

4   How Dogs Learn

How do dogs learn? Very easily, if we teach them properly.

If dogs do something that brings them reward, it increases the possibility that they will do it again. If they do something that does not bring them reward, it increases the possibility that they will not do it again. All animals learn through, or perform for, rewards – and that includes us.

There is nothing new about this basic principle. Trainers have been using it for years. The only difference is this: in the past "bringing reward" has been interpreted to mean praise; "not bringing reward" has been interpreted to mean punishment. Praise and punishment are not enough.

You cannot train an elephant to stand on its hind legs by saying "good elephant" as a way of rewarding it. You cannot train a killer whale to jump out of the water when you blow a whistle by saying "good whale". So at what point did we take the view that saying "good dog" was sufficient reward to increase the possibility of a repeat performance?

Would you put in a second week's work for your boss if, at the end of the first week, all you received was a pat on the back, a smile and the words "good human"? You might, perhaps, if you thought there would be a possibility that you would receive your reward at the end of the second week, but that is because humans have the ability to think things out logically. But as soon as you realised that there was going to be nothing other than verbal praise as a reward, you would say, "Do it yourself, boss." If you wouldn't, give me a call; I've got a job for you,

Over the years, many "old wives' tales" have evolved around the world of dog training and as author and tutor of a correspondence course on canine behaviour, I know from my students' research that these "principles" are still generally accepted.

"If you tell a dog to do something, you must make it do it straightaway."

"You must never use food to train a dog; that's bribery. It must do it because you have said so."

"You cannot start to train a dog until it is at least six months old." (Many dog clubs will not accept a dog for training under six months.)

"If you are going to train a dog properly, you must use a choke chain." (I saw a dog trainer on a Saturday morning children's television programme, showing a chain and saying this verbatim. It would seem that we are now passing on to the next generation what we learnt from the last.)

These are just some of the basic guidelines that I was first taught when I entered the world of dogs. So, based on this knowledge, this is how I tried to teach my first dog how to retrieve a dumb-bell and what, with hindsight, I now see I actually did teach him.

Step 1. I told him to "Sit" alongside me. When he did not obey immediately, I pulled up on his lead and choke chain and pushed down on his haunches.
I thought: I'm teaching him to sit.
The dog thought: I don't like that sit word; it means he's going to push me about.
Step 2. I told him to "Stay" and threw the dumb-bell. When he went after it, I checked him firmly and repeated the word "Stay".
I thought: I'm teaching him not to go until I tell him.
The dog thought: He doesn't want me to go after the dumb-bell.
Step 3. I told him to "Fetch it" and ran with him on the lead to where it had landed.
I thought: I'm teaching him he can go for it now.
The dog thought: Now I'm really confused: he just said don't get the dumb-bell.
Step 4. I pointed to the dumb-bell and told him to "Hold it". When he picked it up, I ran backwards gently tugging on the lead to get him to follow me.
I thought: I'm teaching him to pick it up and bring it back.
The dog thought: I must be allowed it; I'll pick it up. Oh no; he's pulling me away again; I had better drop it.

Step 5. He dropped it. I told him "No", put it in his mouth, and held his jaws together telling him to "Hold it".
I thought: I'm teaching him not to drop it.
The dog thought: Now he seems to be getting cross. As soon as he lets me spit it out, I promise never to chase it again.

I do not need to labour the point. I admit, I may have exaggerated a bit, I was not such a bad trainer. (Perhaps I should have asked my dog what he thought.)

What I was trying to do was to train my dog to perform a retrieve as a complete exercise, before I had taught him what was required from each individual step. Later on I will tell you how I taught my latest dog to retrieve a dumb-bell, but before I do we need to examine the various things that affect a dog's ability to learn.

NEGATIVE THIGMOTAXIS

Now that is quite a scientific sounding pair of words and well worth dropping into the conversation in the pub one day. It simply means that if you apply physical pressure to any animal, it will result in counter-pressure. Think what happens if someone takes hold of your sleeve and starts to pull you; your immediate reaction will be to pull back.

That applied pressure invites counter-pressure is a fact of life and one that we have to accept. If we are going to use pressure to push or pull a dog into any position, the dog's initial reaction will be to resist. If you push a dog into a down, it will initially start to push up. It will also think about pushing up – exactly the opposite of what you are trying to teach. To overcome this resistance, we must then apply more pressure.

Might it not be easier to use a technique that did not involve any pressure, thus removing an obstacle that prevents easy learning?

TOUCH SENSITIVITY

Because of selective breeding, some breeds are less sensitive to pain than others. Terriers for instance and the fighting breeds are usually fairly insensitive. But even within each breed, touch sensitivity varies from dog to dog. You can test your own dog's sensitivity by taking hold of the webbing between the second and third toe on a front foot with your finger and thumb. Start to squeeze gently but with increasing pressure, counting from one to ten as you do. Stop the moment you get a reaction. The lower the number reached, the higher the sensitivity.

How can this affect your dog's ability to learn? Insensitive dogs are not going to respond to some training techniques, whilst the same techniques used on a sensitive dog can destroy the dog's confidence in you as a trainer.

If the dog is involved in a particularly pleasurable activity, then it is likely to be less sensitive than usual. A dog in full flight after a squirrel is not likely to feel the whip of young branches as it charges through the woods. Of course, the opposite is also true. The less the dog likes what it is doing, the greater its sensitivity is going to be. A highly sensitive dog being taught something that it may not be enjoying should be handled with "kid gloves", or – better still – a way should be found of increasing the enjoyment so that you lower the sensitivity.

SOUND SENSITIVITY

The effect of noise can be crucial when you are trying to teach a highly sensitive dog.

Ask a "Sheltie" owner. I have yet to come across an owner of a Shetland Sheepdog that did not train his/her dog in a quiet and gentle manner. Such owners do this out of necessity because they have usually learnt the folly of trying to do the alternative. That is fine if you own a breed that has a reputation for being sound sensitive, but dogs do vary, and yours could be unexpectedly sensitive in this way. Training a dog in a dog club environment with a dog of this type can tremendously affect its ability to learn. You may be aware of your dog's sensitivity and creep around in soft-soled shoes, whispering your commands, but if the guy behind you is clumping around in studded "Hunter" wellies, screaming commands to his half-deaf gun dog, then he is going to turn your dog into a quivering wreck, totally incapable of learning anything.

This of course would be easy to spot, but, like touch, sound sensitivity varies from dog to dog and if we are not aware of its effect on the dog that we are training, then we might be placing yet another obstacle in the path to easy learning.

SIGHT SENSITIVITY

The Border Collie is the classic example of a sight sensitive dog. Border Collies have eyes like radar screens and can spot the slightest movement. Obviously, trying to train a dog like this in an environment where there is a lot of rapid movement is not going to help the dog concentrate on what you are trying to achieve.

There is also something else peculiar to such dogs. Because this is a breed that is generally quick to learn, many people find that their dogs start to anticipate what they are going to tell them to do. This ability enhances their reputation of being "born trained". In fact, in most cases, the Collie has spotted an inadvertent movement prior to the command and has reacted to that: the uncrossing of its owner's legs prior to getting up to take it for a walk, or a glance at the clock prior to feeding time. A well-trained Collie often will come back, as soon as you turn to face it – before you call it. An untrained Collie equally might run away, as soon as you take the lead out of your pocket prior to calling him in the park.

All of these things tend to suggest that Collies have the ability to read our minds. They cannot, but sight sensitive dogs very quickly pick up on the smallest body signals that we transmit prior to doing anything. If we are not aware of our own dog's sight sensitivity, we are likely to tell it off for doing something that we have inadvertently told it to do. It will only take three or four consecutive negative reactions from us, before the dog will refuse to obey the command that we do want it to obey. Then we get cross.

Your dog does not have to be a Collie to be sight sensitive. Many dogs are, regardless of breed, and if, as a result, we are giving confusing signals and then scolding them for obeying, it is no wonder that some clash of values and a lot of misunderstanding arises.

MENTAL SENSITIVITY

Many dogs, regardless of breed, become extremely sensitive to their owners' moods. I feel sure that some readers who are married will have seen their dogs "head for the hills" if a domestic argument breaks out. Mental sensitivity is very closely linked with the dog's ability to handle stress. If we are upset with our dog's performance, a sensitive dog will notice this and the performance will probably get worse.

When I was in charge of training police dog handlers, I could often pick up across the training field negative vibes coming from the handlers if their dogs were not responding in the way that they thought they should. With the more sensitive dogs, this made their performance worse. As a result, a vicious circle was created. My cure for this was always "Put your dog away and go and have a cup of tea." This never cured the problem, but at least it stopped the handler making it worse.

Mental pressure from the handler can have a tremendous effect on a highly mentally sensitive dog. The pressure might be because his dog is not responding as quickly as a colleague's dog, or he has been told to get the dog trained or get rid of it. He might even be feeling "one degree under" or worried about how he is going to pay his mortgage that month. These things have an effect on the dog's ability to learn.

This sensitive type of dog is more likely to suffer from anxiety-related problems when left on its own – house-soiling, destructiveness, howling, barking etc. This is because it is so reliant on its owner, and seeks confirmation at every step of the way that it is doing the right thing. With this type of dog, a scowl, a tut, or even eyes pointing towards heaven can destroy its self-confidence.

I well remember one owner who had done just this.

"I've qualified my English Bull Terrier for Crufts," he complained, "but she tucks her tail between her legs when the judge approaches."

(Every year, without fail, I get calls from show people who have qualified their dogs for Crufts. Even as I write this, my wife has just taken a similar call from someone with a Saluki who has qualified her dog for this show and it carries its tail high and it should be low. The venue where it wins apparently is very hot and her dog does not like it. As a result it carries its tail low. What does she want me to do? Make her dog sad about showing?)

This dog was the sweetest English Bull Terrier that I have ever met. When I first saw her, she looked at me and almost said, "Oh look, a human". She approached me very readily and happily with all the body postures of a dog who respects me as the superior animal. The owner immediately pointed out the fact that her tail was down and it should be carried high. The problem was: according to the breed standard, the English Bull Terrier should be the gladiator of the show ring. The way that it walks with a swagger, because of its shape; its square looks; its egg-shaped, almost bullet looking head: all are designed to give the appearance of strength and confidence. Being the gladiator of the ring, does not of course mean that it has to enter with the intention of fighting anything else that enters. It only has to give that impression through its self-confident demeanour.

In short, this dog was so tuned in to people and especially to her owners that she displayed perfectly normal canine body postures to signify her acceptance of rank. This did not please her owner, who had other ambitions for the dog – ones that she would never be able to understand. Unfortunately, this ambition for the dog was actually having an effect on how the dog was showing because he transmitted despondency whenever the dog displayed anything other than an agressive posture. This despondency upset the dog, who had lost its self-confidence, and only increased its submissive body posture to show him so.

I can honestly say that this is the only one of my clients that I have ever argued with. His dog was regarded as just a tool for his use to promote his personal ambition. Given another handler, I am sure this dog would display the confidence that her present owner was sapping from her.

Mental sensitivity is therefore relevant to both dog and owner. We should not only examine the type of dog that we are responsible for; we should also examine what type of person *we* are before we start our training.

BREED SPECIFIC BEHAVIOUR

We have already discussed some of the behaviour relevant to specific breeds. Collies learn very quickly because they pick up on signals that we do not always intend to give. Shelties are usually sound sensitive and therefore are usually treated very gently. Guard dogs guard and hunting dogs hunt. Yet, far too often, we treat dogs simply as dogs, regardless of what our forefathers bred them to do.

I frequently get calls from owners who tell me that their dog's barking is causing their neighbours to complain. When I ask what type of dog they have got, they tell me that it is a German Shepherd. If they do not want their dog to bark, they should have got something like a Basenji, not a dog with the highly developed guarding abilities of the German Shepherd.

Some breeds herd; some breeds chase; some breeds guard; some are bred as lap dogs; some are bred as gun dogs. Each breed has its own peculiarities and the training should take account of this. If it does not, we might be trying to teach a dog something with a method that is totally alien to its intended role in life. Unfortunately, the training that is available in the majority of dog clubs up and down this country is pretty well standardised. This is regardless of each particular breeds specific behaviour. In the dog clubs that I am invited to visit, it is not unusual for me to hear the same advice being given to the owner of a Saluki, as is given to the owner of a Labrador when it comes to the retrieve exercise. Obviously, with the latter breed the exercise is totally natural, with the former, it is totally alien.

At the end of the day, the effect of pressure, touch, sound, sight and mental sensitivity together with an awareness of breed specific behaviour, must all be considered before any training programme is embarked upon. If we do not take these areas into consideration, the learning process will be affected.

As each and every dog is affected by one or more of these, how are we ever going to be able to teach our dogs anything in a way that they are capable of learning easily?

The answer lies in Positive Reinforcement.

5 The Art of Positive Reinforcement

The following pages will describe a method of teaching that can be applied to any animal but particularly suits the dog. It is a system that relies wholly on inducements and rejects any form of force or physical manipulation. It is a method that children can use. It does not require any natural skill at training dogs. It does not rely on tone of voice, timing, regular practice or any of the traditionally accepted theories of training dogs. All that are required are two things: a brain and a piece of food.

Let us look at two different methods of teaching your dog to go and lie down in one particular corner of the room.

1. We can whip it when it goes to any corner but that one, until it learns that the chosen area is its only safe haven.
2. We can give it a particularly tasty titbit in the chosen area and ignore it when it goes to any of the others.

I feel sure that when you read this example, you said to yourself: "Well, that's common sense. What's so new about it?"

Of course, it is common sense. Every dog owner does the same thing on a daily basis in and around the home without consciously thinking about it. For some reason though, when it comes to making a specific effort to teach our dogs something, we put on our dog trainer's hat and revert to the old-fashioned attitude of "You dog; I master. I say; you do."

When you call your dog at home it is generally to feed it, to put its lead on to take it out for a walk, or to show it that you have dropped some food on the kitchen floor and you want it to clean it up. In fact we rarely call our dogs to us at home just for the sake of calling them; it is usually for a specific reason, and in most cases it is rewarding to the dog. As a result, few people have recall problems at home.

In the local park, however, it is a completely different matter.

You walk around the park with your dog running free, playing with other dogs, chasing squirrels, rooting through the rubbish bins whilst you walk about, lost in your own thoughts. At the park gates, you take the lead out of your pocket and then call the dog to take it home. It is not surprising that so many dogs take one look and then head in the opposite direction. At which point you say to yourself, "I must get that dog trained."

You *have* trained it. You have successfully trained it *not* to come back to you. How? Because the dog quickly learnt that not coming to you is rewarding: it gets a longer walk. Coming to you is unrewarding: it gets taken home.

If you had applied your home training recall methods, by calling him at the gates of the park, giving him a titbit and then going round again, you would soon have your dog responding to your recall command like a bullet.

Bribery? Common sense, I call it.

I often have to smile to myself when I receive a call from people who have a problem with their dog and I suggest that they try rewarding the right behaviour, instead of thinking about ways of punishing the unwanted behaviour, and they reply: "You mean *bribe* him?"

I find it amusing that something to which scientists, psychologists and behaviourists have attached fancy names like behaviour modification, operant conditioning, behavioural psychology and so on, is still regarded as bribery. What really matters is that, applied correctly, reinforcement works: it changes the behaviour from unwanted to wanted.

There are certain underlying principles which govern the successful application of positive reinforcement as a training technique but before we start to apply these principles (or laws) to specific dog training exercises, we should examine each stage, what the purpose of each stage is, and what the learning effect will be. I could make this very boring by giving each stage its scientific name, such as stimulus control, behaviour extinction, displacement behaviour, successive approximation etc. – but I shall not. If you want to go into the techniques in more depth and on a more scientific level I suggest that you visit the psychology section of your local library.

All we are concerned with is how positive reinforcement works and how we apply it.

How it works

First of all, we should forget training exercises as a whole. All that we are interested in to start with is the first move in the right direction. As I have used the example before, let us assume that we are going to teach a killer whale to jump out of the water.

We blow a whistle (the command), and wait. Then we wait a bit longer, and quite often a bit longer still.

Obviously, the whale initially has no idea what is required from it when it hears the whistle, so we have to wait for it to stick its nose out of the water for whatever reason. At that exact moment, we blow the whistle again and give it a fish. When it swims below we blow the whistle again and wait. This procedure is kept up until the whale reaches the *Ah-Ha!* level. "Ah-ha! When I hear the whistle, I get a fish."

This level of understanding is not confirmed until you get a ten out of ten immediate response to the whistle. Until then, the training should not progress further. Although, at the early stages of training, things do not appear to progress very quickly, it is vitally important, if the training is to be successful, that each stage is completed to the total level of understanding. If this is done, you will find that as each stage is entered, the whole business of forming the initial response into a recognisable series of movements snowballs very quickly.

We now enter a stage of the training known as Shaping. What we need to do is change the whistle/nose appears/fish always routine to a whistle/whale leaps clear of the water/fish sometimes routine. It is done in the following way.

Shaping behaviour means that we take one small step in the right direction and move it one step at a time towards our ultimate goal, reinforcing each step as we go until it is guaranteed before moving on. It is an interesting phenomenon that any particular behaviour that is trained to a guaranteed level for reward can be improved upon by withholding the reward.

Let us assume that we have a guaranteed response from our whale that when we blow our whistle ten times, its nose will appear immediately ten times. On the eleventh time we say: "Not good enough, you're not getting the fish."

Now it is almost as if the whale thinks: "But I always get a fish. Perhaps someone pinched it before I got there. I'd better get a move on next time."

The result is that on the twelfth whistle, you get a quicker and more forceful response which causes the whole head to appear. That definitely earns a fish, but from then on that is the only thing that does.

We are now going to establish a whistle/whole head appears/ fish reward routine to our ten out of ten standard before moving on to the next step. As each step is taken, the subject seems to understand what is wanted quicker and the snowball effect takes place.

I deliberately used the example of the whale to make the point that the whole learning process can be achieved without any physical manipulation. We initially wait for the right step in the right direction, reward it, guarantee it and then shape it.

Q.   What's the difference between that and bribery.

A.   Bribery is where you use the reward as a lure to encourage a movement. Reinforcement is where you reward a volun- tary movement.

Q.   Do you always have to give the reward?

A.   It works better if you don't. Once the behaviour is guaran- teed, only the biggest, quickest and most impressive response is rewarded. Sometimes, six or seven shaped responses will have to be completed before one reward is forthcoming.

Q.   Does the reward have to be food?

A.   It can be anything that the subject views as worth perform- ing for. It would be no good trying to shape my behaviour with a plate of cabbage. I hate cabbage.

How we apply it

In the last chapter, I told you how I attempted to teach my first dog how to retrieve. Now I will tell you how I taught my current dog to perform the same exercise.

My first dog took a few weeks to learn and never really performed the exercise in any great style. He was a German Shepherd, a breed renowned for its trainability. My current dog performs the same exercise with a twinkle in her eye and incredible speed for a dog of her size. She is a Japanese Akita, a breed renowned for its stubbornness.

I spent a lot of time on the training field, over a period of weeks, teaching my German Shepherd. I spent a few minutes a day, over a period of a few days, teaching my Akita, and I never got out of my chair.

Using these techniques, I have recently helped a police dog handler to achieve the same results with his German Shepherd. In fact, we took the dog from completely untrained to Home Office standard in less than the usual time and with far better results than with traditional techniques.

My dog's name is Yoko. Get it? John and Yoko. She was fifteen months old when I decided to teach her the exercise. Although I no longer have the time to compete in the sport of working trials, I do still judge them, and it was a chance remark by a competitor that prompted me to teach her to retrieve. The remark was: "You will never teach an Akita to retrieve properly." I thrive on challenge.

I sat at the desk in my office with a tin of titbits next to me. I held out the dumb-bell and said, "Fetch it." Yoko sniffed the bar and I said, "Good girl", then gave her a reward.

The first session lasted about five minutes and she received approximately 60% immediate reward for immediate responses. The others were eventual rewards given for the correct responses, but only after having sniffed the desk, pawed at me, barked at me, or tried a variety of different responses to get the reward. On the next session the same day, the *Ah-Ha!* level was reached. She positively nose-butted the dumb-bell whenever I gave the cue.

The shaping on to the next stage took a little longer, and over the period of four sessions, each of about five minutes, she tried various different things to get the reward. The ratio was probably 15%, 25%, 70%, 100%. What I was asking from her now was not that she nose-butt it, but lick it.

When I refused to reward her for licking the dumb-bell, I was lucky enough to hit a learning curve (the snowball effect) much earlier than I expected. She positively snatched the dumb-bell away from me and looked at me as if to say: "Look, stupid, I am touching it . . . gimme the food."

No one can predict the pattern that an exercise will shape. We might have a structured order in our minds, but we have to be governed by the speed that the animal dictates. Once you have rewarded a particular movement, then that is the only movement you can reward until it is established. Yoko took a greater leap forward than the one that I had expected from her and because I had rewarded it out of enthusiasm, I had to wait for her to do the same thing again. It took less time than I thought, but then she is a very greedy dog.

After having made this quantum leap forward, the whole exercise shaped very easily. Within no time at all, I was throwing the dumb-bell on to the settee at the far side of the office. She was fetching it on command and sitting in front of me with it in her mouth as proud as Punch.

On the first occasion that I attempted a competitive type retrieve outside, I would have given her ten out of ten. But then I suppose I am biased.

Let us now take two simple movements: the SIT and the DOWN. Using the same aforementioned methods, let us see how it is possible to teach a dog to respond to these commands, using a "hands off" method that is guaranteed to be successful. To speed up the process, we need to resort to bribery. In other words, we show the reward to encourage the movement. As soon as that level of understanding is reached, we revert to voice command only and wait for the right movement to happen. Then we shape it.

For the SIT, show a titbit, even touching it on the dog's nose. Say "Sit" and slowly move the titbit above and slightly behind the eye line.

The structure of the dog is such that if the head goes up and backwards the bum must go down.

For the DOWN, select an obstacle that your dog will need to reduce its size considerably to get under. It will depend upon the size of your dog. For example, a coffee table might suit a German Shepherd. Place the dog on one side and offer a titbit under the obstacle to the dog. As it goes to take it, slowly withdraw the titbit under the obstacle, encouraging the dog to follow and giving the command "Down". The moment its belly hits the floor, hand over the reward.

With a little bit of forethought, you can teach your dog to do anything that you want it to do. It can be done incredibly easily, incredibly quickly and in a manner that your dog will enjoy.

If we can teach our dogs to do what we want them to do, all that is left is to stop them from doing the things that we do not want them to do.

To achieve this we use a system of negative reinforcement.

6 The Art of Negative Reinforcement

Negative reinforcement is something that your dog does not like, but it is very different from the traditional training methods.

In the past, physical punishment has generally been used to correct unwanted behaviour: a sharp tug on the choke chain; hitting the dog with a rolled up newspaper; grabbing it by the scruff of the neck and shaking it. These are just some of the popular methods of trying to teach the dog that you are not pleased with its actions. The problem is:

1. The majority of these methods are usually applied too late: either when the dog is right in the middle of the act or, in most cases, after the act.
2. The punishment comes directly from the handler; so the dog quickly learns to do what it wants to do and then avoid the handler.

I am sure that we have all seen the dog on a lead that shows aggression towards another dog and then cringes down with its eyes turned up towards its handler. It has not learnt *not* to show aggression; it has only learnt what the next stage is. Clearly the punishment did not fit the crime. It fitted the cessation of the crime. In other words, the dog does what it wants to do, then shows submission because it has been caught.

The human view of punishment is really very strange. Bank robbers are much the same as dogs. The type of person who is capable of robbing a bank is not ·deterred by the threat of punishment. He just takes care not to get caught. Yet if, as the robber started to plan the robbery, a policeman knocked on his door and said, "We know what you are thinking and we will be watching you," he would change his mind at that very minute. That is not punishment. It is negative reinforcement.

With negative reinforcement, the trick is to get the dogs to believe that it was *their* action that brought about the unpleasant circumstances. A classic example would be if your dog were just investigating the rim of your neighbour's dustbin lid and thinking: "That smells tasty, how do I get to it?" and if at that precise moment your neighbour threw a bucket of water on him from an upstairs window, I guarantee he would never go near your neighbour's dustbin again.

The essential element is that it was apparently nothing to do with you, or your neighbour for that matter, providing he said nothing when he threw the water. Shouting and applying negative reinforcement alters the thought patterns and centres the dog's attention on to the reinforcer. It then becomes punishment. This is one of the most important principles of what is basically "aversion" therapy. If you can leave the dog's attention 100% on the act, the aversion is 100% effective. If you distract it by 20%, you reduce the effectiveness by that amount and so on.

The circumstances under which I would use negative reinforcement would be where there is a learned and self-rewarding behaviour pattern: chasing tendencies; aggression; jumping up; excessive barking etc. However, I would not use it before I had considered all other areas that might be affecting the dog's behaviour. (Take away the root cause and quite often there is no problem left to control.)

I would also have decided on what alternative behaviour I want the dog to exhibit. All too often I hear of advice being given on how to stop a particular problem, with no advice having been given on what the dog should do instead. It is very easy to stop a dog doing *this* if you make *that* more rewarding.

In my practice, I use a variety of different techniques, none of which involves pain, punishment or direct confrontation to stop a dog behaving in an unwanted manner. Over the years I have found the use of sound to be the most effective. To this end, in 1984 I researched and developed "Dog Training Discs". These simply consist of a series of small brass discs which create a sound that, because of the introductory conditioning, can be used to interrupt the dog's thought patterns and focus its attention on to the owner, who then tells the dog what to do instead.

The technique is loosely based on an old practice first recorded (to my knowledge) in a book called *Training Dogs: a Manual* by Colonel Konrad Most. He recommends something called a casting chain, a light metal chain about a foot long, or alternatively a throwing stick. He states that these aids should only be used when the dog's attention has been distracted from his master and when he is at some distance from him, so that he does not see where it comes from. The moment the stick or chain strikes the dog, the master should call the dog to him. It worked on the principle that: *You might be 40 feet away from me, dog, but I can still get to you.*

As a young impressionable dog trainer, I often used the casting chain technique and it invariably worked. However, as I am a rotten shot and anyway quite often the dog would turn and look at me just as I threw the chain, I was never able to understand why, if the dog saw me throw the chain which usually missed it by a mile, it came back to me when I called it. The psychology behind what was happening appeared to be all wrong: if someone was throwing something at me, I would put as much distance between me and them as I could.

It was some years later that I discovered the answer. I was helping a vicar to train his young Dobermann bitch and he was struggling to push her into a down position to which she was resisting almost to the point of panic. As I called out to him and moved forward to stop him pushing her, I took my hands out of my pocket and a chain fell out. As it hit the floor, the bitch stood perfectly still. I then told the vicar to tell her gently, "Down". She responded immediately.

I was amazed at what had happened, but I pretended that I did that sort of thing every day. I now tell people that the vicar comes to see me on Sundays because of what he thought was a God-like power over animals. Who am I to destroy his faith?

It was basically at this point that I reached my own *Ah-Ha!* level of understanding. What was happening with the casting chain method has nothing to do with the ability of the handler to reach and reprimand the dog from a distance. It was the effect of the sound that was the key factor, regardless of where it came from. As a result, I spent the next few months researching the use of sound to control and train dogs.

I specify "to control and train" because used correctly this form of training can be used, not only to interrupt unwanted behaviour, but also to reinforce verbal authority.

Many trainers who think they understand the technique have said to me that they can get the same results with a chain or a bunch of old keys. I am also receiving more and more reports about one trainer who is using a chain inside a child's wellington boot, and of another who throws walking sticks at dogs. All of these methods are based on the Konrad Most principle of long distance punishment. The sad thing is that I saw a Jack Russell bitch a few days ago who was petrified of me, because she had been hit by a chain-filled wellie, thrown by one of these trainers and as a result was now frightened of all strange men. According to the owners, until this point she had been happy, outgoing and over-friendly with people. It was this over-friendliness that was causing the problem. The trainer's noisy wellie had hit the dog on her rear end for no apparent reason; she was not doing anything wrong at the time. This treatment had turned her into a quivering wreck in the presence of strange men. A few weeks earlier, I had seen a client whose dog's eye had been damaged as a result of being hit by a walking stick thrown by the other trainer.

For my own part, having advertised "Free dog training to research a new technique" and being inundated with hundreds of dogs of various ages, breeds and problems, I discovered that what was vital to the success of the method was how the sound was first introduced to the dog and that it must be unique in that it was only every heard when it related to the behaviour that the dog was engaged upon at the time. In other words, things like chains, keys, wellington boots and walking sticks are all associated with taking your dog for a walk. If the sound has a two-fold effect on the dog (both positive and negative) then its aversive effect will quickly disappear.

According to many of my clients, the Discs work like magic, but there is no magic involved. The following extracts from unsolicited letters show the wide range of purposes that they can be put to.

I now just have to rattle the Discs if she is about to start barking and she is silent instantly. The great bonus, to my mind, is that this does not "flatten" her – she still bounds about but doesn't have to drive me mad with her barking. – Mrs F., Hampshire.

A friend from France, staying with us recently, was intrigued and impressed by the use of your Training Discs and has asked me to send her some. Our lives are certainly more peaceful and only occasionally are the Discs needed. – Mr. O., Wimbledon SW19.

Certainly they are proving very effective against my dog's habit of jumping up and a couple of other minor faults. Congratulations, I thought she would never learn. – Miss M., Surrey.

British Telecom had to dig a hole in the garden to repair our phone. Beck would "help"; so I gave them the Discs. She stood and watched instead. They are worth their weight in gold. – Val M., Bolton

I find the Training Discs work quite magically. With their help, I (at long last) can get him to lie down on command from 50 to 60 yards away which is terrific. – Rosemary M., Devon.

The secret to their success is:
1. It is a sound that is unlike any other.
2. They can be picked up and carried in your hand or pocket without them making a noise, enabling the owner to produce the sound at the right psychological moment.
3. They are used neither as a missile nor as an extension of the owner's anger, but purely as a reaction to an unwanted action. If they were to be misused and thrown directly at the dog, they are light enough to cause no pain or damage (unless a particularly deranged owner threw them in the dog's eye, but then anyone who would do this, would do it with anything).
4. The introductory conditioning technique, which is carried out away from the problem that you are trying to cure, tunes the dog into the sound as being one which has the desired negative effect.

I introduce the Discs to the dog in the following way.

I call the dog over to where I am sitting and offer it a titbit, telling the dog to "Take it". I repeat this procedure three or four times and then, without saying anything to the dog, I make a movement of placing a titbit on the floor. As the dog follows my hand, I first chink the Discs and then throw them alongside where I am placing the food. Then I immediately remove the food and the Discs. The whole procedure is done in one movement very quickly. I continue to speak to the owners, totally ignoring the dog. Quite often I am not even able to let go of the food; some dogs are very greedy. In general, the majority of dogs do not pay any attention to the sound of the Discs at this stage and many of them continue to sniff about the floor trying to find the food that they think is there.

I repeat the procedure of giving food with the words, "Take it" each time, and then go to place some on the floor again. There is a chink as the dog follows my hand and I throw the Discs again if the dog follows to the point where I want to place the food. It is immediately removed, as are the Discs. The dog is again ignored as I continue my conversation with the owners.

The whole purpose of this procedure is to teach the dog that it can take the food that I offer and say it can have, but if I choose to put *my* food on *my* floor, then no greedy "chow hound" has any right to take it. The slight chink that I produce is the warning to back off; the louder chink and the arrival of the Discs is the reaction to the dog's action of trying to take the food. Ignoring the dog afterwards is my way of saying, "It had nothing to do with me. That was your own stupid fault."

The majority of dogs go from ignoring the Discs on the first occasion to walking away from the food on the floor and lying down next to their owner on the fourth occasion. Some dogs learn quickly, some do not learn at all (but not many). As with any training technique, it does not suit every dog.

Although the initial purpose of this introductory procedure is to condition the dog to the sound as an aversive stimulus, the canine learning process goes a little bit deeper. What I am saying to the dog is: "You can have the food that I do not want and say you can have, but *do not consider taking any food that is in my possession or in my vicinity.*" I am claiming one of the basic canine privileges that all dogs know is afforded only to higher ranking animals.

I usually further increase the effectiveness of the Discs with one more exercise. This one also relies on the dog's basic instinctive knowledge that higher ranks have certain privileges: "If I occupy the entrance to the den, do not push past me."

I stand up and walk towards the door. At the same time I tell the dog in a very matter-of-fact way, "Stay there, doggo." I do not want to use any compulsive dog training tones. I do not want to hold up the finger of doom that is constantly pointed at the dog; above all, I do not want the usual pregnant silence that most dogs recognise as meaning everyone is paying attention to me so I will wait until they are distracted and then I will do what I want. As I open the door, I am talking to the owners.

Naturally, out of the corner of my eye I am watching what the dog is going to do. A half step towards the door means that the dog has no intention of staying. The Discs are thrown in the doorway and the door is shut. Nothing is said to the dog and the conversation between myself and the owners is carried on. By this time we are usually only saying "Rhubarb, rhubarb". (It is awfully difficult to find something to talk about when your attention is being diverted and you are trying not to let it show.)

After a couple of repeat exercises, the dog either takes a half pace back, sits or lies down – any one of which is immediately rewarded. Then you can usually be assured that it has made its choice. One option is to push past you, which it finds unrewarding. The other is to make a clear indication that it will not do so, for which it is rewarded. It's a dumb dog that does not soon learn the difference.

You will no doubt have realised by now that although the technique is different, the criteria are exactly the same as discussed in Chapter 3.

Providing the dog responds in the expected way, as a result of this sound aversion conditioning, the negative/positive reinforcement principles can be applied to almost any behaviour problem that is not being influenced through any other factor. Here is a typical case (initially taught on a long line or flexi-leash for safety): There's sheep, let's chase. Hear a chink; let's not. Oh look; I get rewarded if I don't.

The small percentage of dogs who do not respond to the proper introduction of the Discs, I usually find will respond to a similar introduction to something like a personal rape alarm. This is a gas-filled canister with a whistle attachment that emits a high pitched shrill sound. It tends to be fairly limited in its use because it relies on the frightening effect of the sound as opposed to the learning effect of the Discs. When, for instance, I use the Discs on the first occasion, most dogs do not respond because the learning effect is gradual and it builds slowly with each progressive use. When I use the shrill alarm, the result is usually immediate. However, this is a fear-induced response, and that ideally is not what we are looking for. Understanding the rules is what living with dogs is all about. For this reason, I tend only to use the fear induced sound aversion therapy, when the immediate alternative is euthanasia; for example, sheep chasers who have a predatory intent, who live in sheep country (so the problem cannot be avoided), and who have not responded to the Discs.

It is interesting to note that in the years that I have been using sound to interrupt unwanted behaviour, very few dogs have failed to respond to one or other technique.

On a few occasions, I use taste as a deterrent, especially for dogs that chew specific objects like electric cables. Dogs that chew electric cables are running the risk of getting very seriously dead. (You would be surprised how many of them do, especially puppies.) For this, I use a product called Bitter Apple, which is non-toxic but tastes absolutely horrible.

Obviously, spraying dangerous items such as exposed cables makes putting them in the mouth a negative experience to the dog and extinguishes the problem. Where the problem is non-specific chewing, and assuming the problems relating to anxiety and teething periods have been taken into account (see the Problem Solving A to Z), the following procedure has proved successful in the past.

If, for instance, your dog is chewing the legs of your Queen Anne table (which to the dog is only a bit of wood) the cure has to be extremely unpleasant to the dog if you want success to be guaranteed. You will need a spray bottle of Bitter Apple, two tissues and a cheap perfume.

Spray one of the tissues with a very watered-down version of the perfume and the other with Bitter Apple. Offer the dog the perfumed tissue and as soon as it smells it, pop the Bitter Apple tissue into its mouth holding it shut for a few seconds – definitely not nice.

Next, take a favourite but disposable toy that you know your dog will pick up as soon as it sees it. Spray it with Bitter Apple and leave it somewhere accessible. A few inches in front of where your dog will approach, spray a watered-down solution of the perfume. Your dog will approach the item, take note of the cheap perfume and either remember the previous experience, or totally ignore it. Either way, the smell will register.

If it goes to grab hold of the toy, it will very quickly spit it out and run around the room spitting and spluttering. This toy can now be thrown away and replaced with something else.

Your watered-down perfume can now be sprayed a few inches in front of anything that you want to protect. The popular items should also receive a spray of Bitter Apple. The idea is that you give your dog an olfactory signal that to continue with the present course of intended action is going to be bad news. Because the perfume is watered down, in no time at all the smell disappears so far as we humans can detect. The dog, of course, has an olfactory ability something like 100,000 times more powerful than ours. As it approaches the intended chewable victim, it notices the trigger scent. Based on past experience, the dog thinks, "Not on your life!" and backs off.

All of these negative reinforcers (except for the shrill alarm) have a trigger cue to the dog: "Off", where it is verbal; "Chink", with the Discs; and weak perfume with the Bitter Apple. The whole concept of negative reinforcement is that the enforcer should be absolute, the warning should be clear.

Part II
The Positive Approach to Problem Behaviour

7   Training "Problems" for Owners

To say that training can affect behaviour would seem to be a contradiction in terms.

For the moment, let us put out of our minds the idea of training "The Woodhouse Way", and let us look at how we usually try to teach dogs not to display particularly obnoxious behavioural traits. For many years now, the attitude has been that the way dogs learn is through a series of rewards and punishments. In fact I recently presented a paper at Cambridge University for UFAW (Universities Federation for Animal Welfare) and on the front cover of their draft copy for the symposium programme it was stated that, "Training animals involves a series of praise and punishment". In fact, they did not actually put this statement on their final programme, but their initial thoughts reflected years of indoctrinated beliefs.

Whenever I come across a trainer who has this type of old-fashioned view I usually ask the question, "Could you train a killer whale to jump out of the water when you blow a whistle if you punished it every time it refused to comply?" From a human point of view the same principles apply. If you are trying to learn a particular concept and every time you get it wrong you are punished, before long you will decide that the concept is not worth learning in the first place and, given the opportunity, you will probably avoid the lesson.

What follows is a classic case history which describes how the praise/punishment syndrome can have a negative effect on what we are trying to teach our dogs.

Donner is a Rottweiler who was brought to see me by a middle-aged couple from Leicestershire who owned her. Mention a "Rottie" and a picture is immediately conjured up of a very macho dominant male. Not so in this case. This was a very friendly two-year old bitch of impeccable breeding. She had been branded as a fighter/killer because of the following circumstances.

Donner had been introduced into the house at eight weeks old to replace the previous family Rottweiler who had died of old age. One of the members of the household was an adult Border Terrier dog, who, from day one, resented the intrusion of the new arrival and took every opportunity to put her in her place. The attention Donner received as a pup did not help, and the writing was on the wall as soon as Donner started to mature. There were frequent battles between the two of them over points of possession with Donner exhibiting a typical Rottweiler guarding and dominant attitude and the Terrier behaving like a never-give-in Terrier.

The result was that when Donner was about twelve months old, a fight occurred, which resulted in the Border Terrier being found with both its back legs almost severed and its intestines exposed. The veterinary surgeon had no option but to put it to sleep.

From that day Donner was regarded as a rogue dog and treated that way in the presence of other dogs. The local dog club advised the owners: "Each time she even looks at another dog, lift the choke chain up behind her ears and 'neck' her." A length of hosepipe, brought down sharply on top of her head, was another suggested remedy.

As the months progressed, Donner became more difficult to control near other dogs; consequently, her walks were becoming less frequent. The point had been reached where the decision was: either cure her or put her down.

I approached the problem on the assumption that Donner was not a fighter. The incident that had branded her as such was an environmental situation between two dominant characters. To take this approach involved reversing the entire way that Donner was being treated. We did this in the following way.
1. The choke chain was replaced by a broad leather collar.
2. The usual short lead was replaced by a strong extending lead.
3. I fitted her with a lightweight muzzle specially designed for such breeds, allowing them to pant and lap but making biting impossible. This would allow Donner to interact with other selected non-aggressive dogs without any danger of her attacking these dogs.

4. The level of off-lead control that the owners had over Donner was increased by use of the Discs.
5. Her diet was changed to one designed to have a calming effect upon her (see Chapter 8)

The leather collar meant that she did not experience pain or discomfort every time she even saw another dog, and the increased freedom of the extending lead meant that she did not have to approach every situation at the speed and limited distance set by her owners. This took away any need for defensive aggression. It also allowed contact with other selected dogs without danger. This, in turn, allowed the owners to relax, which eliminated all handler-transmitted tension. Through the use of the Discs, rather than force, she became more attentive to the owners and much quieter as a result of the short-term change of diet. Within a few days, the owners were able to see Donner's true temperament, which was outgoing, boisterous, but friendly.

The initial consultation had lasted almost three hours and during this time we had discussed canine communication and body-language. This new awareness showed them that Donner would readily show submission to a more dominant dog. The muzzle was soon discarded. (It was only a short-term solution.) Donner was allowed to interact with other dogs in general and no problems arose.

The owners wrote to me, telling me that the family now has a new Terrier puppy. "Initially the puppy snapped at her, but Donner took it in good part. By the end of the evening the puppy was making advances. Now the relationship is developing along very acceptable lines. Donner is the boss but she is also a close companion. The two have glorious games and Donner is definitely making up for the fact that she never had a dog to play with as a puppy." Letters like this are so rewarding to me. Donner's owners were considering having her put to sleep but she is now a very much loved and important member of the household.

Another case history which nicely highlights the fact that sometimes the way that we train dogs can have a detrimental effect upon them is one of a black Belgian Shepherd (Groenendael). This was a well-bred, perfect specimen of the breed, who had turned aggressive. None of his brothers and sisters, nor either of his parents ever showed any aggressive tendencies.

Therefore it came as some surprise to the breeder that this dog, Samson, had bitten at least six times – and always in doorways.

He was brought to see me, by the breeder, from the kennels where he was staying in Bristol, because the kennel maids could not handle him. The breeder, who had taken him back from the original owners and put him into these kennels, was convinced that Samson was not an aggressive dog.

The circumstances were that she sold him to people who seemed sensible but had never owned a dog before. After much deliberation, she decided that provided she could keep a watchful eye upon them they would be suitable owners. Apparently at a very early age the dog had become very pushy in doorways, especially with the woman, and neither she nor her husband had sought advice from the breeder. Instead they had asked advice from so-called experienced dog people who had told them that they should put Samson on a choke chain and lead, and the moment he tried to push past them through a doorway they should lift him clear of his feet and drag him to a tying-up point, where he should be horse-whipped! Understandably, this did not prevent Samson from pushing, but he did become aggressive in doorways whenever they were approached while he was on a lead. The natural progression was such that, when doorways were approached, the lead was tightened in anticipation of any displays of aggression.

I witnessed the dog's so-called aggression. It took the form of jumping up and crossing its front legs over the lead, with the eyes rolling to show the whites: a classic fear response. This was read by the owners, and subsequently by the kennel maids, as the onset of aggression and it was met by aggression from them. What they did was to trigger off a fight or flight reaction. Samson could not run away and was fearful of the situation. He had no other recourse but to defend himself. It was to his credit (in dog terms) that all the bites were inhibited (bruising, grazing, etc.). If I were Samson I would have panicked so much I would have torn the people to pieces, but then I am a coward!

We put Samson on to a broad leather collar and flexileash (much like the previous example), to increase the critical distance and sense of freedom. I approached the entrance to my office with Samson and he immediately panicked and backed off about six feet, which this type of lead allows them to do. I continued to walk in saying, "Don't be silly, come on", but not trying to force or drag him in. He responded by trotting in, and was rewarded with a titbit. Over the next thirty minutes or so we did this on three or four occasions until Samson was quite trustful about going in or out of the doorway on leash. What we were doing was starting to alter a learned experience, which had resulted in an aggressive response to a form of training which is peculiar to humans – that of punishing unwanted behaviour in order to teach the dog not to do it again. Desensitisation is the word that has been coined for this technique which sounds awfully scientific but basically means that we change the dog's expectations of what is about to happen.

I mentioned that we did this until Samson was quite trustful, and that is the key to this particular form of aggression. Samson, understandably, had lost his trust in what people were going to do to him in doorways when he was on a leash and choke-chain.

To cure him completely will require a very understanding owner and one who, in the future, can recognise the difference between fear and aggression, uncertainty or stubbornness. My personal opinion is that the kennel maids do not have the time or sufficient trust in the dog to cure him. The breeder herself is in such circumstances that she cannot keep Samson on a long-term basis at her own home. I fear that, in the end, Samson will have to face euthanasia. This upsets me because basically he is a nice dog and his behaviour is simply the result of advice given to his novice owners, with the best possible intention and for the best of possible reasons. This kind of advice, however, is wrong and has to be changed for the future good of all dogs and the future safety of owners.

All too often dogs are put down or labelled as aggressive because of the training techniques adopted. Both these case histories show that punishment as a form of training actually intensified the problem and pushed normal canine behaviour into an area where the dog had become dangerous. Dogs bite, growl and bark, but that does not necessarily make them aggressive dogs. They also use aggression as a form of dominance and they respond to us as other members of their pack. Therefore, on occasion, they may show aggression towards us in order to try and dominate, or discipline us. How we handle that situation will either make or break the relationship that we have with our dog. If we consider the fact that a dog can use its jaws four times faster than a human can use his hands, then we can begin to understand that if we have allowed a dog to reach a situation where it genuinely thinks it is higher ranking and we openly confront it in an aggressive way, we are likely to get bitten.

If we challenge a dog on a point of discipline in such a way that the dog has no way of showing a flight response, then the dog is going to defend itself. I do not condone these bites but at least I do understand them.

In Chapter 12 I shall be discussing training in much more detail, and there it should become even more obvious where training affects behaviour. At this point what I am trying to get over is that we know exactly what we are trying to teach our dogs, but all too often we do not know what the dog is learning from the experience. Another case history might help to put the whole thing in perspective.

I recently received a phone call from a lady who stated that her nine-month-old dog was still house-soiling overnight. After asking her about diet, exercise times, times of feeding, etc., I asked what she did when she came down in the morning and saw that her dog had soiled. She replied "I don't punish him. I do not believe in smacking dogs. All I do is rub his nose in it, and make him go outside." She genuinely believed that this was the standard method of training dogs not to house-soil, but all the dog learns from this experience is that humans have a fetish about dog mess. They seem to come into a room looking for it and if they find some, they home in on it with eyes as black as coal and with blue sparks coming out of their ears, roaring those immortal words, *"What's this?"*

The dog, already frightened by the owner's physical appearance, cringes at the tone of voice and adopts a submissive posture, which, when it was a baby with its mother, it had learned was the way to stop further hostility. Not so with humans it would seem. It is grabbed by the scruff of the neck and its face is pushed into the mess and it is isolated outside for a long time.

From the human point of view, what you effectively do is to force excreta up the nostrils of the dog and into the fibres of your carpet. From the dog's point of view, what you effectively teach is that the presence of a mess on the carpet and a human at the door is bad news.

If I were a dog who had active defence reflexes, I would then growl and bite to defend myself, and I would probably be called an aggressive dog. If I were a dog who had passive defence reflexes, I would run and hide at the first aggressive facial signal from the owner, and they would probably say that I knew that I had done wrong. If I were a clever dog, I would realise that the combination of my stool and my owner was bad news, so I would probably eat the stool. I suppose that they would classify me as a coprophagiac.

Whatever my character, however, I would certainly be wary of defecating in front of my owners, because I would have learnt that they seem to have a strange fixation about dog mess so, if they are all dressed up to go out and they take me for a walk on a lead in the rain for my last 'poo', they are going to get pretty wet because I am not going to perform in their presence. I will wait until they are out of sight or I might even go in another room so that they cannot find it.

Provided the dog soils away from his nest, then that is normal canine behaviour. The ways in which we try to teach the dog that his habits are not acceptable to humans can have a profound effect on our future relationship and how the dog behaves in general. (See Fouling and House-Soiling in Problem Solving A to Z.) However, if we start to take a "think dog" approach, it all begins to make sense.

8   Stress "Problems"

We recognise stress in people as a cause of ill health. Doctors believe that in general practice stress is a major factor in about 70% of the cases that they see. In some practices, particularly in the inner city areas, the figure has been put as high as 80 to 85%. Stress drains the body's immune system, leaving it open to all kinds of infection, and re-stocking the body's stress pool reservoir is a very slow process.

Prolonged exposure to stress can play a causative and "trigger" role in killer diseases and it is also linked to major emotional diseases – depression, anxiety, chronic tension states, and the more serious mental illnesses.

Many of the stressful situations that arise today are largely of our own making. Our lifestyle is such that we search for better and higher-paid jobs to enable us to afford more luxury goods. That often means travelling greater distances to get to our place of work, which invariably means that on a twice-daily basis we either compete for room on the roads, travelling bumper to bumper like a herd of cattle walking nose to tail, or are packed like sardines into the various forms of public transport available to us. During these regular journeys, not only are we constantly on the alert to try to improve our position in the herd: watching to see which lane is travelling the fastest, and then trying to manoeuvre ourselves into that lane; trying to gain a seat, or the best position near the door so that we can be first off and clear of the mass of people at the ticket barrier. Our personal space is invaded all the time, and we tend to ignore the people that we travel with, because we are usually forced too close to them for our own comfort, and by ignoring them we are fooling ourselves that they are not there.

At work, everything is urgent and everyone thinks that they are indispensable. Communications are such these days that letters are only written to confirm telephone conversations. Everyone wants everything right now. Documents are faxed to avoid delays in the postal system or to avoid lengthy telephone calls, yet ironically people still ring up to make sure that the fax was received. More and more people are walking around with portable phones because they have to be contactable at all times; if they are not, someone else might step in who can be contacted and take over the job. We are all living in a rat race that is getting faster by the day and it is resulting in both physical and emotional stress. Although doctors sometimes prescribe drugs to relieve the symptoms, almost always they urge patients to take a holiday so that they can get away from the root cause.

Dogs cannots take holidays, but they also suffer from stress. The difference is that they do not bring it upon themselves. It is largely a knock-on effect of our own lifestyle and is probably the major reason why there is a need nowadays for canine behaviour therapists like me, whereas we were not required a few years ago.

Not so many years ago the average pet owner only had one car, or none. The children used to be walked to school by Mum and the dog went along as part of its daily exercise. During this walk it was stimulated by the different smells it encountered, it got used to long periods of on-leash exercise, and it socialised with adults, children and other dogs. Quite often it was tied up outside the shop whilst Mum picked up the odd item of shopping.

Nowadays, most children are driven to school by Mum in the family's second car, which is often a hatchback or estate so that the dog can sit in the back. After dropping the kids at school, the dog might be driven to the park where it is allowed to jump out (off leash) and run around, usually only for however long it takes to relieve itself. Then it is back into the car and home, or to a multi-storey car park whilst Mum shops in the supermarket complex.

Our modern way of living, and the pace at which we live it, does affect our dogs' quality of life, and as a result we have behaviour problems.

Lack of mental and physical stimulation, as well as an increasing number of dogs who are lacking companionship – it is only recently that it has become normal for both husband and wife to work full time – will eventually cause the dog to become stressed, resulting in stress-coping behaviour such as tail chasing, pacing, fence running etc.

The problems arising from confinement are being tackled by

zoos and sea life parks, and an increasing amount of research is being funded to devise activities for animals kept in such places to enable them to satisfy their instinctive needs to forage or hunt. It is a sad fact that whilst advances are being made to improve the lot of captive wild animals, the domestic dog is heading in the other direction.

To suggest to owners that a lot of their dog's problems could be solved if they were to leave their portable phone at home and take the dog for a nice long walk, with plenty of opportunity to engage in normal off-leash activities, seems too simple to be the real answer. With an awful lot of dogs, it is as simple as that. Unfortunately, I am often faced with the type of owner who protests that they just do not have the time and tell me that the dog has a big garden to play in all day. My reply is usually quite blunt. "The size of his prison does not impress him, or me, one bit. If you cannot put some time aside for your dog, you shouldn't own one."

In Chapter 2, I mentioned the problems caused by puppy farming. Sadly, I am seeing more and more of these. The lengths that the dealers go to in order to disguise the puppies' true origins are incredible. Puppies being delivered directly to the house supposedly because the breeder wants to 'check out' the home; whole litters being looked after by caring people who are doing it for a friend whose bitch died giving birth and many other seemingly genuine reasons why the prospective owner cannot see the mother of the pups. On the other hand, there is the pet shop trade where the new owners are told that the caring and knowledgeable pet shop proprietor is only selling the puppies for a customer, or where the name of the store is "so well known" that people automatically believe that the puppies must be the best bred and the most well-cared-for pups available. Most of these are just fronts for the loathsome trade of puppy farming and dealing. With the dealers paying the farmers around £25 to £35 per pup and selling them for around £150 to £250 per pup, depending on the breed, it soon becomes obvious why it has become such big business.

To be fair, the majority of people who are engaged in this sort of "breeding for profit" business are not cruel people – they just have a complete lack of knowledge about the critical periods of development of the dog. Because the problems arising from this type of early upbringing only manifest themselves later, the breeders are quite often not aware of the problems that they have created. It is also quite significant that, at the time of writing, the government is considering tighter controls on problem dogs. As the appendix to this book will show, 25.6% of the problem dogs that I saw over a twelve month period had problems related to lack of proper early experience. Due to tighter EEC controls on grazing animals per acre, the Ministry of Agriculture suggested in 1982 that farmers turned their outbuildings into kennels and farmed dogs, they even offered an advisory service on how to do it and Wales was the area that was the most affected by these controls. The Welsh puppy farms have now become notorious amongst enlightened dog people as a major source of problems in dogs. It is vitally important that the average family pet owner is made aware of the importance of obtaining puppies only from reputable breeders.

It would be unfair to accuse everyone who has a litter of puppies for sale, and no mother to show to the new owners, of being a dealer. There is however one vital clue that helps to confirm any suspicions.

A common denominator with many dogs from puppy farms is an early history of severe gastro-intestinal infection, pneumonia, or hepatitis. These problems are usually brought on through the physiological and psychological trauma of being crated and transported. The cold, vibration, inadequate food and water, but mainly the fear of being confined, cause stress. A normal puppy's stress reaction is a defence mechanism involving the production of certain hormones from the adrenal glands (ACTH or adreno-corticotrophic hormone). As previously mentioned, because of their lack of proper early socialisation these puppies have inadequate stress reactions. They quickly become exhausted and more susceptible to disease.

After such "transportation stress" and lack of proper loving care on arrival, these puppies usually develop some infection within two weeks. By then the dealer has sold the puppy and, whereas buyers may send back a defective electrical appliance, they have usually become too emotionally attached to the puppy to even consider sending it back. Anyway, most owners tend to blame themselves for the pup becoming ill. It is only when the pup becomes ill within a few hours of arriving at its new home, as can sometimes happen with the added stress of the extra journey, that the new owners tend to take issue. If they accept the replacement that is invariably offered, it is quite likely that it also will develop problems. It is also quite likely that the dealer will have the sick puppy destroyed: paying out on vet's fees for a number of weeks is going to eat into their profits.

So far, we have discussed two causes of stress; one which manifests itself in psychological and behavioural problems and the other which causes physical problems. But by far the most common form of stress is the one caused by owners who inadvertently load too much responsibility on to the shoulders of their dogs, as described in Chapter 3. These dogs are carrying responsibilities that they are not genetically equipped to cope with: in a feral dog pack, they would not be the Alpha figure. The human analogy would be the person promoted to a position of responsibility that he could not cope with. He would much prefer someone else to make the decisions. In time, the stresses of the job cause him to be irritable, bad tempered and possibly ill.

The stress of ultimate responsibility is recognised as a major factor in human ill-health and inappropriate behaviour. The same applies to dogs. I see such dogs on a regular basis. They come into my office with their owners and immediately assume a leader role. Once I have established my rank every dog of this type, without exception, settles down and goes to sleep. In effect they take the holiday they so desperately need. They are no longer stressed or frightened. They are just relieved of all responsibility, and as a result they become calm and contented. The ability to handle the stress of leadership is genetically inherited, not thrust upon you. In most cases, by relieving these dogs of the responsibility it automatically makes them nicer dogs and many owners make that comment.

In the adult dog, stress manifests itself in two different forms: positive and negative. It is how these behaviour patterns are interpreted by the owner or trainer that will dictate whether or not the dog will become more, or less, stressed.

I have mentioned the trainer at this point, because the type of stress that we are now going to discuss is typical of the stress that is evident in far too many training clubs in this country today. So how do we recognise the fact that a dog is in stress, as opposed to the dog that is dominantly saying, "I won't"?

It is my opinion that anyone who advertises that he, she or they, run dog training classes and charges a fee for that service –

even if that fee is only 50p – has a responsibility to be as knowledgeable in that area as it is possible to be.

Any sensible person would not pay for riding lessons unless their instructor was at least qualified to the level of BHSAI (British Horse Society Assistant Instructor), nor would they have an unqualified farrier to shoe their horse. Any sensible person would not buy a house that was built by anyone other than a member of the Master Builders Federation. They would not take their dog for medical treatment to anyone who was not a qualified vet. So how is it that Mrs Bloggs, who has probably done fairly well with her "born trained" Border Collie at local exemption shows, can advertise as a dog training instructor? It is because there is not enough awareness amongst the general pet owning population that there are good training classes and bad training classes.

In fairness to the majority of Mrs Bloggs in this country, they genuinely believe that they are doing a good job. They often do it for little or no reward and with a fervent desire to help other people to train their dogs properly, because they like dogs. What some of them do not understand is that dogs are not machines – because their Collie responded to a sharp check on the choke-chain, dogs like Rottweilers, Dobermanns, German Shepherds will not respond in the same way. When they do not; they tend to blame the owner for not doing it properly. Thankfully, the time is fast approaching where proper qualifications are being made available to the truly dedicated person, and in time, I hope, the pet owner will seek out qualified and knowledgeable instructors.

What the instructor should be looking for in his/her class is the dog that is incapable of learning because it is exhibiting signs of stress. These are clearly recognisable to the informed and aware instructor in the following way:

Negative stress
This will take the form of: dilated pupils; ears back; panting or salivating; sweaty paws; lying flat on the floor in a total freeze posture; excessive hair loss; and, in severe cases, submissive urination. There is only one cure, and that is to remove the dog from the environment and to distract it quickly with some pleasurable activity. To take the view, like so many trainers do, that the dog will just have to get used to it, is as negative as the

stress exhibited and will have the opposite effect on the learning process to the one that was intended.

Positive stress

This is much harder to recognise and easily attributed to disobedience – the standard diagnosis in most dog clubs. The only way to tell one from the other is to have been in a position where you have observed the dog over a period of time. The "disobedient" dog is more likely to behave in the same way all the time. The "stressed" dog will suddenly start behaving like a hyperactive puppy when you start to insist that it performs in a particular way. It will run around in circles, it will invite you to enter into play behaviour with front down, bum up postures, and the more you try to regain control, the sillier it becomes. It will become almost impossible to catch and if you do, it will continue to act in a manner that ranges between submission and hyperactivity. Again, removing the dog from the stressful environment is the positive cure. Alternatively, changing the training attitude will help.

Stress is recognised as a cause of both physical and psychological problems in humans, but with dogs we tend to take the view that they have no emotions; that they are just machines and that, if we say "You do", they will. We should remember that the reason man and dog have got on so well together for more than 10,000 years is because our social structure and values are so similar. The most remarkable case of stress I have ever encountered showed just how similar they are.

One day I received a phone call from a lady who told me that her dog acted very strangely whenever she had visitors.

"What breed of dog is it, and what does it do?" I asked.

"It's a three-year-old Jack Russell called Jenny, and she licks all the time that visitors are here and even when we visit other people."

I told her that it was not unusual for very friendly dogs to lick people and she replied: "She doesn't lick people, she licks walls."

Her vet could find nothing medically wrong with the dog and it was he who had suggested that she contact me. After a lengthy conversation, during which I found out that it was not just walls, it was also chair legs, table legs, coffee tables etc. that Jenny licked, we made arrangements to meet.

Both the husband and wife attended the consultation and, sure enough, within a few minutes Jenny started to lick the walls. What was worrying was the frantic energy that she put into it. From the moment that I received the initial call, I assumed that I knew why she was behaving in this way: Jenny must be attention seeking. What I was now witnessing seemed to confirm my suspicion, but how wrong that proved to be.

I told them to ignore her, so as not to give her the attention I thought she was looking for. Next we tried various aversive techniques – all of which resulted in one thing: she got worse. Throughout the consultation, the husband sat comfortably back in his chair and said nothing. It was as if he were only there as the chauffeur.

I had asked both on the phone and again at the start of the meeting whether there were any other circumstances that might trigger off a similar display and had been assured that there were none. It was only when there was a third person in the room and it did not matter whether Jenny knew them or not.

At this point, the woman left my office to get something from the car. As soon as she was out of earshot, her husband said: "She's lying you know. The dog does it all the time except when she's on her own with me."

Sure enough, Jenny had stopped licking and just stood there looking totally exhausted.

"It's her voice," he said. "It makes her act like one of those new-fangled flowers that wiggles to music. When she talks, Jenny licks. I've told her, but all she does is argue with me and won't listen. Her mother's the same – voice like a damn fog-horn."

I almost heard the penny drop in my mind. What I was dealing with was a stress reaction to domestic disharmony. They did not need me; they needed a marriage guidance counsellor, but how was I going to tell them?

"I only agreed to come if she promised to leave the room for five minutes so that I could prove it to you. When she comes back, Jenny will start licking again."

Sure enough, just as he predicted, Jenny resumed her frantic licking behaviour almost as soon as the woman re-entered the office.

What she had done on her visit to the vet, and subsequently to me, was to invent a set of circumstances that triggered off the wall and furniture licking, namely the presence of visitors. What was actually happening was that Jenny was being used as a buffer between the husband and wife, a sort of focus for arguments. A change in the environmental situation and time are the only cure for this sort of problem.

In the past, I have known dogs that have displayed very bizarre behaviour during domestic upheaval. Probably the most common being the onset of house-soiling. It is not unusual to hear about dogs that defecate on the bed under these circumstances. On one occasion, the dog defecated on the kitchen table.

This case history just goes to show how deeply our dogs relate to us as individuals and as pack members. They may not speak our language or, more to the point, we may not always understand theirs, but the attachment between man and dog is more than between man and any other animal and in some cases that includes fellow men.

A colleague of mine at the Woodthorpe Veterinary Group, Richard Bleckman (who is also a veterinary adviser to the APBC) recently asked me how often I had suspected that the behaviour problems that the dogs exhibit are as a direct result of the owners that they live with. "In far too many cases," was my reply. His concern was that over the past few months he too was beginning to see a direct link between owner pressures and actual physical ailments in their dogs.

The problem that we are both faced with is: how do you even start to suggest to an owner that their dog would not act in such a manner, or would not be ill, if they themselves changed their outlook on life?

9   Diet "Problems" – The Clues

"You are what you eat," is a very old and a very true saying. There are not many people who are unaware that some particular foods, or an ingredient in the food, can affect the health or the behaviour of some individuals. Some drinks can have the same effect – the non-alcoholic variety, I mean; we are all aware of the effects of alcohol on behaviour. Different people react to different things in different ways. The same is true with dogs, but rarely considered.

As far as I am aware, there has never been a properly-commissioned scientific study on the effects of diet on the behaviour of dogs, although one of the leading pet food manufacturers is funding a residency at Edinburgh, with a major project looking at "food allergy". Various veterinary surgeons and leading behaviourists have published papers on diet-related allergies. Where such an allergy exists, the behaviour of the animal would certainly be affected, but, as with people, every dog is unique. It would therefore be quite difficult, if not impossible, to come up with concrete evidence that a particular food or ingredient definitely affects the behaviour of all dogs. We shall see.

I must state at this point that I am not a nutritionist. However, the advice that follows is based on experience of diet therapy with literally hundreds of cases over the past few years. As far as I am concerned, the results that I have achieved have proved conclusively that diet therapy cannot be ignored by anyone involved in the business of advising owners on how to cure their wayward pets.

I intend to divide this subject into two different areas. This chapter is really to promote awareness. Perhaps when you read it you will be able to say: "Ah-Ha. My dog does that. Perhaps I should try a diet change." Chapter 10 will be a little bit more technical and is designed to give the "Ah-Ha" owners a bit more information to work on. If you have not said "Ah-Ha" after Chapter 9, you do not need to read Chapter 10.

My first real breakthrough with diet therapy came a few years ago when I visited a client who had what she described as a hyperactive three-year-old male Gordon Setter called Rolly. Hyperactive was not the word. Rolly practically ran around the ceiling with excitement when I arrived, and continued to act in an over-the-top boisterous way until my client told him to lie down. It was interesting to see that he did in fact obey her – a result of many hours of private dog training lessons – but all the time he was lying down he trembled uncontrollably. The trembling could be ignored if you did not look at him, but the howling that accompanied the trembling could not – not even by the neighbours. I was told that he would keep that up for the entire duration of his "Down – Stay" exercise. I did not want to see whether he would or not: I could not stand the noise myself any longer. When she released him from the "Stay", he resumed his over-friendly, but definitely "yobbish", behaviour.

The owner was an air hostess, working on the short-haul flights between Heathrow and Glasgow, and she was allowed to take home all the left-over steaks when the galley was restocked. Rolly was on a pure steak diet.

As Rolly was trained, inasmuch as he knew what position to adopt to a particular word of command, all that was left for me to do was to slow down his activity level. I advised a natural diet (see Chapter 10). The results were incredible. A few days later, I received a phone call saying: "I would have called you earlier, but we initially thought that Rolly must be ill. Within twenty-four hours he was so calm that we could not believe that it was just the change in diet. Now we know that he is not ill; he is fit, well and active when he needs to be. The problem was his diet."

In this particular case, it was easy to spot the fact that the diet was a high protein, red meat diet that was incorrectly balanced. It did not contain enough energy-giving ingredients in the form of fats and carbohydrates; therefore most of the protein was being used as an energy source. Not only might this contribute towards hyperactivity, but it can also result in a loss of condition. The amino acids from protein are required for tissue repair, growth and other physiological functions. If the benefits obtained from the protein source are robbed to supply energy requirements, the results can be disastrous for the dog in terms of health and behaviour. Contrary to popular opinion, high protein diets are not necessarily bad, but the balance between protein, fats and carbohydrates should be taken into consideration and weighed up against the dog's daily energy needs. With Rolly, the *balance* was wrong. A working dog, or a pet dog that gets lots of energetic exercise will need different energy/protein requirements from a pet dog that is of the "plodding" variety.

The advertisements on the television make it sound so easy . . . "Give your dog a tin of this and he will perform miracles, and be your friend for life. Not only that, he will also prefer this to the one advertised before and the one coming on next . . ." The pet food industry is a multi-billion pound market and each manufacturer is obviously out to get the biggest slice of the market. The priority is to get a food on the market which looks good from the human viewpoint. That requires chunks of what looks like real meat in what looks like real gravy – soya and colours can do this very effectively. The dog must prefer it to all others – that requires spices and flavour enhancers. The price must be as low as possible – that means that the ingredients must be cheap in the first place. Cheap usually means poor quality.

This does not mean that a food which looks good, is liked by your dog and is reasonably priced is a bad dog food. However, it may not be doing your dog much good. There are a number of clues which will tell us whether it is worth trying a change in diet or not.

The following is my twelve point questionnaire, designed to establish whether there is a need to change the dog's diet and how urgent that need is.

1. Is your dog usually in good health, or does he/she have persistent digestive problems, or regular allergic reactions to fleas, grass etc?

2. Does your dog regularly suffer from flatulence?

3. Are his/her motions inconsistent in quality: sometimes loose, sometimes firm?

4. Is the stool volume quite large and invariably quite smelly?

5. Does your dog eat greedily but never appear to put on any weight?

6. Is the activity level unacceptable, either way?

7. Does your dog drink an awful lot of water?

8. Does the hair and skin look healthy, or does he/she constantly suffer from hair loss?

9. On a ritualistic basis, does your dog scratch behind the ears, or on its chest and abdomen; chew at the root of its tail; nibble or lick its feet and legs; rub its eyes and nose with its feet or rub its head along the carpet?

10. Is it always eating grass, shredding twigs or digging up roots in the garden?

11. Does it pinch tissues and toilet rolls, or, if it is destructive in some other way, is the object of its destruction invariably fibre based?

12. Does your dog eat its own excreta?

Any one of these symptoms on its own could indicate something other than a diet-related problem. For instance, it is quite possible that your dog does have a flea or grass allergy. Difficulty in absorbing food would explain the stool quality, stool eating etc., and is not always diet related. Weight problems could indicate worms. The dog may enjoy chewing up sticks. It may be destructive in an effort to relieve anxiety (covered in Chapter 15). However, the more "yes" answers there are, the more chance that a change of diet will be beneficial.

So what exactly is the relevance behind each of the symptoms on the list, and how does it relate to diet?

The following is not a medical diagnostic chart; it is merely a list of possible causes.

1. Allergic reactions. Could be because the body's defence mechanisms are permanently in action, fighting some allergen in the food. Any extra attack on the body is the straw that breaks the camel's back. Remove the food allergen and the body can combat the rest.

2. Flatulence. Could be because the food is not being properly digested in the small intestine. Undigested food in the large intestine will trigger off a fermentation process and a subsequent build up of gas. Too much soya in the food can produce the same effect.

3. Inconsistent stool quality. Another indication that the food is not being digested properly. Fermentation irritates the

lining of the intestine, and an irritated bowel does not absorb water very well. Hence it is lost in the stool. The dog will drink more water to compensate.

4. Large, smelly motions. Usually a direct result of undigested, fermented food.

5. Failure to put on weight. Obviously, if your dog is not getting the right nutrients from the food he is going to be very greedy and bolt it down with no visual beneficial effect.

6. Hyperactivity/low activity. As mentioned at the start of this chapter, the balance of the food is a key factor not only to the health, but also to the energy levels of your dog.

7. Excessive water intake. Might indicate excessive intestinal disturbance.

8. Coat and skin vitality. There is a possibility that the protein is being utilised for energy with a subsequent loss of health and vitality. Vitamin/mineral deprivation will have the same effect, but in my opinion a good and well-balanced diet should not have to be supplemented.

9. Ritualistic scratching and licking. This could indicate that there is an allergic reaction to the food, or to an ingredient in the food. If the body's defence mechanisms are in action, this will in turn trigger off cells which release histamine into the body. In the dog, these cells are located in their greatest number on the feet and legs; around the ears, eyes and nose; on the root of the tail and on the chest and abdomen. Frantic licking or scratching of these areas, especially shortly after eating, will eventually damage the skin and leave it open to infection.

10. Eating grass, twigs and roots. Sometimes an indication that the food is not being digested properly. Dogs are vomiting animals (they are capable of regurgitating unwanted or unpleasant food), and intestinal fermentation will encourage them to eat grass as a means of rejecting the cause of the fermentation. Alternatively, the diet might be deficient in certain minerals. Some grasses contain minerals, and the body instinctively tells the dog that it needs them. The chewing of twigs or the search for roots could indicate that there is also an instinctive message being sent that the digestive system needs more fibre. This can be difficult to

prove scientifically, but I find that changing to a better diet reduces the behaviour.

11. Tissue stealing and fibre-based destruction. Could be another indication that there is a craving for fibre to help the digestive process in some way. Tissues are the finest form of pure wood fibre.

12. Eating its own excreta. Might indicate that the food is not being properly digested. If the nutrients are not being extracted, the stool is as nutritional as the original food and as far as the dog is concerned, well worth eating. Disgusting to us, but perfectly normal and sensible behaviour to the dog. If this behaviour continues however, consult your veterinary surgeon.

I would estimate that well over 50 per cent of the dogs that I see in my practice exhibit behaviour patterns that are being influenced to a greater or lesser degree by their diet. (*It should be noted that I specialise in behaviour problems, and I am not suggesting that over 50 per cent of all dogs are affected.*) In a few cases, the change in diet was all that was necessary to resolve the problem; in others, it made the rehabilitation of the dog much easier and quicker.

There is another factor to consider: more and more pet food manufacturers are including ingredients that are designed to keep the dog fit, healthy and full of energy. Of course this is important and something that the caring pet owner would take into consideration when buying a particular brand, but, as previously mentioned, the way that we live with our dogs today is very different from the way that we used to live with them.

If you feed your dog like a prize fighter or top athlete, it is going to need an outlet to utilise the energies induced by these diets.

Ideally, we should be feeding our dogs with food that is sufficiently nutritious for their own particular energy needs – and no more. Believe it or not, this does not mean that every owner should be a qualified nutritionist. Observation and common sense are enough.

10   Diet "Problems" – The Facts

If you intend to read this section, then it is quite likely that, at some point during Chapter 9, you said to yourself, "Ah-Ha, perhaps it might be worth trying a diet change", or maybe you are just interested in going into the subject in more depth. The following is an extract from a trade magazine called *Pet Product Marketing* dated June 1987. It was written by David Shaw, and was headed "Good Food Costs More".

> Very few owners know the value of the pet food which they purchase. If it looks good to the owner and the pet eats it, it must be right. The pet owner never eats it and has no way of judging value or quality. The only guide is the analysis on the bag – 20% Protein, 4% Oil, 3% Ash and a few vitamins. Exactly what does it mean? Not always a lot. Most dog owners think that 20% protein must be better than 18%. What they do not realise is that you can get protein (20%) from dried nettles, lupins, brussel sprouts and of course soya. You can even get it from old boot leather. Do you know what 20% is?
>
> A huge amount of dog health problems are caused by bad nutrition. This leads to vet bills and not too happy customers. One of the biggest problems is lack of dietary fibre – not the figure on the bag which is a laboratory analysis, but a sufficient amount of good, natural roughage for a dog's stomach to get hold of.
>
> A dog is mainly carnivorous by nature and thousands of years of domestication will not change that. Its digestive system is designed to eat carcasses including hair, skin and gristle and fat, not a continuous diet of slushy meals.
>
> As human beings, we have the same problem caused by eating too many things which are ground to powder before being used for food.

Protein is equally important. To put it simply, protein is made up of amino acids, some of which are suitable for dogs and from which they can extract correct food value. Others are not. Meat-based protein which suits dogs and cats is expensive, is bought by all manufacturers on an open market, and there is no such thing as cheap good dog food.

If a manufacturer wishes to produce a cheap dog food he has to cut down on the very ingredients which suit a dog's digestion the most. In other words, you pay for what you get and there is no way round that.

The easy way for some manufacturers is spicing and some are expert at it. Very sophisticated spices are now available and so are gelling agents. Sawdust could not only be made to look good, but also to be gulped down by every dog. Add some soya to build up the protein and you have a very suitable protein analysis. An exaggeration, but it makes the point.

So what do you look for? The analysis on the bag is a guide if you understand three things:

(a) The analysis on the bag is the average of everything in the bag. If there are only two ingredients of 20% protein and 10% protein in equal parts, the average must be 15%. If there are 10 ingredients it is again the average over the lot.

(b) If you put more high protein ingredients into your mix, then the average must become higher. But high protein does not mean suitable protein.

(c) In almost every case quality ingredients are more expensive. They are bought on the open market and secret supplies of high quality, cheap ingredients do not exist.

I suppose that this all seems very obvious, but let us go a stage further and look at an actual complete dog food mix and see what happens. And we will look at protein only.

We will mix one part of meatmeal (60% protein), five parts of soyameal (45%) and 14 parts of wheatmeal (10%), TOTAL 20 parts. It is worked out as follows:

PARTS	PROTEIN
1 meatmeal	60%
5 soyameal	45%
14 wheatmeal	10%

MULTIPLY FOR TOTAL PROTEIN

	60
	225
	140
TOTAL	425

Divide the 425 total by the 20 parts and you have 21.5% protein. That will be OK on the bag. In fact, we can get away with 22% or 23% as a 10% leeway is allowed. We have also used a lot of soya to build up our protein and soya is a cheap way of doing it. So you can sell it cheaply.

But not so good. Both soya and wheat have a very low oil level. The average oil in the mix is only 2.3% and a good dog food needs three times that. And oil is a very expensive average to increase.

The one part of meatmeal will make the food palatable (if not we can shove in a bit of spice) but it is hardly a high-quality dog food with all that soya protein. *Dogs are not vegetarians*, and the level of roughage is almost non-existent. If we bake it into lumps it will help the dog's digestion in the short term but sooner or later dogs eating it will end up with digestive problems.

So where have we got to? We have a food which can be made to look OK and we can quote a good protein level. We can put it in a smart bag and sell it to retail very cheaply. No one will query the oil or fibre. Most people mix in a bit of tinned meat or brawn anyway – they can always blame that when the dog looks out of sorts later.

This is exactly what happens. We are all so obsessed with cheap dog foods that quality goes out of the window. Buying ingredients on the open market, no one can produce a high-quality complete dog food and sell it through the pet trade's normal channels, cheaply.

Most important of all, a level of protein means nothing unless you know what that protein is. 18% is enough in a dog food if it is good animal protein. If it is vegetable then 100% is not enough.

The important thing to try and find out from the manufacturer is what exactly is in the food and at what percentages.

If the manufacturer starts hedging and avoids a straight answer in any way, be suspicious. Or stick to manufacturers who have a reputation to uphold in the dog market and who are proud of successes with their food.

Finding out from the manufacturers what exactly is in their food is not such an easy task. It is not unusual for a manufacturer of a complete diet to declare that their food is free of additives and preservatives or contains no antioxidant, if they themselves do not add it. The fact that some suppliers of the raw materials must include an antioxidant to protect their product is not always stated on the label. "Contains no *added* preservatives etc." is a clue that they are probably present in the food, but the manufacturer has not increased them. Similarly phrases like "no additives are used which are not necessary for the nutritional needs of pets" certainly always make me think: "What does that mean?"

It is highly likely that a supplier of fats and oils for inclusion in the manufacturing of a complete dog food would include an antioxidant to stop the fats from going rancid. With the long shelf life of many of these products which contain oils and fats and claim to be free from all added this and that, we can see how easy it is for us to be misled. The question that I ask is, if the product has a fat content, how is it protected?

In his book *Pet Allergies*, Alfred J. Plechner, DVM, writes, "Unfortunately, the public and most veterinarians receive their entire nutritional information from manufacturers whose primary interest is sales. After a study of pet foods during the 1970s, Dr Paul M. Newberne, of the Department of Nutrition and Food Science at the Massachusetts Institute of Technology, had this to say: 'Much of the information on how best to feed your pet is misleading and primarily designed to sell a product, often with very little, if any, supporting evidence to back the claims made by the manufacturer. The pet-owning public and in many cases the veterinary profession has thus been at the mercy of the mass media advertising, often to the detriment of the health of the animal.'" Plechner goes on to say, "There is mounting evidence that a lifetime of eating commercial pet foods can shorten your pet's life."

Although this study was done in the 1970s, the book was written in 1986, and Plechner states, "For years I have been watching the pet food market with great concern and what I see are antiquated and improper formulations full of chemical additives, questionable ingredients that cannot be utilised and inadequate levels of vitamins and minerals. Today's food is daily becoming more inadequate and unacceptable for today's animals. The criterion for purchase is no longer what food is best, but rather what food will cause less problems."

I think that some of the questions we should be asking are: Does "EEC-approved antioxidants, colourants and preservatives" mean that they are OK? If the antioxidant BHT (which is widely used in pet foods) is not permitted in foods intended specifically for children and babies in this country, if BHA is only allowed in the same foods if it is there to protect added Vitamin A, and if these restrictions have been influenced by people who are concerned with hyperactive children, should not warning bells be ringing in the minds of concerned dog-owners?

Having said all that, where does that leave you if, having read Chapter 9, there is a suspicion that it would be beneficial to change your dog's diet?

There are a number of diets that I use regularly depending upon the problem with which I am faced. Over the years I have experimented with various different types of food with varying degrees of success and as a result of this experimentation I now recommend the following diets. These are listed in order of my preference together with my reasons for trying the alternative.

EUKANUBA

This is a complete and balanced dried dog food, with good quality white meat protein. It is also very high in oils and fats.

I feed my four dogs on it and I have done so since it was first brought into the country. It is easy to feed and, because it is so nutritious, the dog needs about half to two-thirds the normal quantity of food. Where there is clearly a need to change the dog's diet, I recommend this food for the following reasons:

1. It has a very high acceptance rate. In other words, most dogs take to it immediately.
2. White meat protein is an easily digestible protein source and one that suits most dogs.
3. It has been developed by canine nutritionists and veterinarians. This means that the dog's daily nutritional requirements

have been studied very carefully. In fact, the makers of Eukanuba (the American-based IAMS Company) make a point of stating that owners should not add anything to the diet in terms of vitamin or mineral supplements because this might create imbalance in the food which would be detrimental to the job that the food is intended to be doing.

Although the IAMS Company state that they have done no research into the behavioural effects of their food on dogs, my own particular records show that the use of this food is beneficial where there is a behaviour problem allied to a diet problem.

The IAMS Company recommend that most dogs be fed on a free-choice basis: the bowl is filled up and the dog is allowed to take from that bowl what it needs. Once your dog gets over the feeling that it must be Christmas every day then it tends just to go to the bowl, take a few mouthfuls and go away. Later on, it will return and take some more. In this way it tops up its nutritional requirements. Although this food is a high-energy type of dog food, dogs do tend to regulate their own nutritional intake, and many of my clients have told me that, when their dog has had a particularly active day, it tends to eat slightly more; when it has had an inactive day, it tends to eat slightly less. There is also a complete range of products available for every dog's stage of development – from puppy, through working, to older dog.

The food does contain two antioxidants. There is a small quantity of BHA to protect the fat from going rancid. (Even so it has a limited shelf life, and should never be bought other than in a sealed package.) The other antioxidant is Ethoxyquin which is in the vitamin pre-mix. Neither of these antioxidants is added or increased by the manufacturers. However, they feel that it would be dishonest not to admit their presence, even though under the present regulations they are not obliged to do so. I find this food particularly useful because, as we shall see, it is a food that can be fed either on an ad-lib, or portion-controlled basis, depending upon the behavioural problem that I am faced with.

I have explained this product in some detail because it is the one I use in most cases. I generally ask the clients at least to try it for about a month, and then to stand back and look at their dog and ask themselves the question: "Is this food doing the job that it is intended to do and does my dog like it?" In most cases, the answer is yes.

HILL'S SCIENCE AND PRESCRIPTION DIETS

The Hill's Diets have been developed by veterinary surgeons and are available only from your vet. They have a range of dry and canned foods, which have been formulated to suit dogs from the initial growth period right through to the senior dog, and this allows owners to pick a diet that suits their particular dog, whatever its age or activity level.

Hill's do state that approved EEC antioxidants have to be used with all dried foods to prevent the fat content going rancid, and this, of course, is perfectly true. Ethoxyquin is the one that they use. Except for the Science diet which is specifically formulated to be "low calorie", this product, like Eukanuba, has a high-calorie density. This means that a reduced quantity will meet all nutritional needs.

The main reason why I recommend Eukanuba and Hill's Diets and try to steer clear of canned food is that, in most cases, something has to be added to canned food. I find that the average pet owner has difficulty in getting the balance right, and balance is the most important consideration when it comes to feeding commercial pet foods. Getting it wrong results in a waste of time for all concerned, but more importantly, it could be harmful to the dog. I would add that there are millions of dogs who are being fed on canned meat and biscuit with no detrimental side effects – I only deal with problem dogs and as the appendix to this book will show, the dog's diet is an area that must not be ignored.

Unfortunately, I am constantly faced with owners' prejudices against complete diets. Their objections are usually based on old wives' tales, or they have been given misguided advice from people who have not known the facts. Perhaps the following will help to dispel the myths surrounding complete and balanced diets.

Probably the most common objections are that either the protein level or the fat content is too high, and that this can cause hyperactivity or lead to obesity. The complete diets that I have mentioned are carefully balanced to assure proper energy and protein metabolism. If fed according to the manufacturer's instructions, these problems do not arise.

Many owners have the attitude that their dog likes variety in his diet. Because humans like egg and chips one day and roast beef with Yorkshire pudding another, they feel that their dog would like the same. In fact, a dog's digestive system is designed to recognise and digest each particular type of food. It then produces a form of bacteria which helps it break down and digest that food. If the food is constantly changed, the digestive system will not have the bacteria necessary for proper digestion, and the result is usually runny, smelly motions. To be fair to your dog and to you, it is better to find the best diet for your dog, and then stick to it.

There are three noticable side effects when Eukanuba or Hill's food is first introduced to your dog on a portion-controlled basis.

1. The dog will appear to be hungry. This is because its gut will take a little time to get used to a smaller quantity of food.
2. The dog will appear to drink more water. This is because the moisture content is usually only about 10%, whereas canned food has a moisture content from 75% to 80%, and your dog will need to compensate for this. I personally think that buying canned food is a very expensive way of buying water.
3. The stool quantity and quality will alter considerably. Smaller, firmer, less smelly motions will be passed and – an added bonus – there will fewer of them.

THE NATURAL DIET

This is a special diet I sometimes use where I still suspect a diet-related problem but the dog is not responding to Eukanuba or Hill's. The contents are simple:

50% cooked brown wholegrain rice. White rice is deficient in nutrients and therefore should not be used. If you boil the rice briefly once, then turn off the heat and let it absorb the water naturally, it will save fuel and also retain the vitamins etc.

25% vegetables. I use mostly green vegetables, but feel free to add different varieties if you like. (Avoid turnips, potatoes or other starchy vegetables.) Parsley-and-watercress mixture from health food shops is a good substitute for fresh vegetables.

25% white meat. Most people choose chicken, but fish is also perfectly acceptable. If you use "human grade" chicken, do not throw the skin, stomach or liver away; add them to the mix. These should be in the same proportion as in a live chicken. Cook or roast the meat thoroughly but not excessively.

If you wish, you can add *in moderation*: sunflower oil, garlic, kelp, bran or natural yoghurt (good for intestinal flora).

Do *not* add: red meat, doggy chocs, treats or snacks, any canned food or biscuits, coloured dog chews etc.

The amount fed depends entirely on your dog's present weight. A good guide would be to start with roughly the same amount of bulk that your dog is used to getting, and adjust it up or down as needed.

The Natural Diet (TND) should be fed half in the morning, half in the evening. It will keep in a fridge perfectly well for three days. You may prefer to make a large batch and freeze it in portions of three days' supply. This is a low protein diet (14% to 15%) which I would use for a short period only to establish whether the problem is diet related or not. Fed longer than three to four weeks, it would require careful vitamin/mineral supplementation.

To ensure that the dog's digestive system is educated to any new diet, it is advisable to introduce the change of food over a four-day period at the rate of 25% per day.

When considering the arguments of high-protein versus low-protein diets for dogs it should have become clear by now that what is important is the quality and the quantity of the protein eaten and how well balanced it is with the rest of the ingredients. It is not enough to switch your dog to a low-protein diet, although this may produce dramatic results within 24 to 48 hours, especially when it comes to taking the "fizz" out of a dog. My experience has shown that where diet is a relevant factor, whether it be in the few cases where diet is the major cause of the behaviour problem, or whether it is a minor factor, speedy results are nice but not what we are looking for.

How to read the label

As from 1992 the labelling regulations for pet foods will insist that the percentages of protein, fat (oil), fibre and moisture in the food be clearly stated on the label. At present, not all manufacturers do so. However, since different pet foods vary enormously in their moisture or water content, it is necessary, in order to compare the true percentages of a given nutrient between different foods, to make a comparison on a "dry matter basis". The water fraction of a diet (which can be over 80% in canned foods) does not contain any valuable nutrient – these are contained within what is known as the "dry matter fraction".

The percentage of dry matter is calculated by subtracting the percentage of moisture present in the food from 100%, but until the new regulations come into force you might have to get this information from the manufacturer.

If we look at two different types of food, one with a high calorie content (Diet A) and the other a lower calorie content (Diet B) we will be able to see how important it is that this extra information is included on the label.

DIET "A"   30% protein; 10% moisture.
DIET "B"   9% protein; 80% moisture.

On the face of it, diet "A" would seem to be higher in protein than diet "B", but if we calculate on a dry matter basis we will see how misleading this can be.

DIET "A"   30% protein; 90% dry matter (minus the 10% moisture).
DIET "B"   9% protein; 20% dry matter (minus the 80% moisture).

As we can see, 33.3% of the dry matter in diet "A" is protein, whereas in diet "B" 45% of what is left after the water content has been removed is protein.

Since dogs eat grams of food, not percents, it is then possible to calculate the actual daily consumption of protein (or any other nutrient group). To do this, we need to multiply the grams of food fed per day by the percentage of dry matter food and then by the percentage of dry matter protein (or whatever nutrient group we are calculating). This formula can then be used to compare dry to dry foods, dry to canned foods or any other combinations.

The calorific differences between diets will determine the manufacturers recommendations on what amounts should be fed each day. One cannot merely look at the percentages on the label and determine the actual grams of a nutrient being consumed by the dog per day. Feeding a low calorie diet with a lower percentage of the nutrient in question may result in a higher daily intake of that nutrient. Let us look at an example.

We will compare a complete dry diet with 30% protein and 10% moisture ("A") against a complete canned food with 9% protein and 80% moisture ("B"), and see exactly how many grams of protein we would be feeding to a Toy Poodle weighing about 10lbs.

DIET "A"   Manufacturer's recommended daily amount, 90g.
DIET "B"   Manufacturer's recommended daily amount, 555g.

Using our comparative multiplication table, let us establish the real facts about these two diets.

DIET "A"   Grams of food per day, 90. Multiplied by the amount of dry matter, 90% = 81g. Multiplied by the dry matter protein, 33.3% = 26.97%
DIET "B"   Grams of food per day, 555. Multiplied by the amount of dry matter, 20% = 111g. Multiplied by the dry matter protein, 45% = 49.95%.

As you can see, the food with the lower protein content on the label, is actually a higher protein diet. It always amazes and saddens me to hear that a client, with whom I have spent a great deal of time considering their dog's nutritional requirements, has gone in to a pet shop to obtain the food that I have advised, only to be told by the person behind the counter that high protein foods are not good for dogs.

It is a fact that some dogs are more suited to one diet and some to another and, contrary to how this must seem, I am not advocating one over the other. I am, however, suggesting that you look at your dog's behaviour, lifestyle, breed and individual character *and* understand how to read a label before you decide on a diet for your dog. I hope the time is approaching when people who sell dog food over the counter will understand the food that they are selling and give the right advice to the people who ask the questions.

CONCLUSION

We should be aware of everything that has been said so far before we decide whether a high or low protein diet should be tried. The long term effect on behaviour and health is what is important.

In some cases, the ingredients within the diet need to be considered and this has been covered in full but, as a reminder, percentages mean nothing if the quality is not good enough, then the dog's health will eventually suffer.

If, after reading Chapter 9, you have decided to try some diet therapy of your own on your dog and are unsure about whether you should try a high or low protein diet, the information in this chapter about how to read the label will help you to determine just what type of diet your dog is already on and this will help you to make a decision one way or the other. However, I strongly recommend that you seek veterinary advice before taking any action.

In this chapter we have been talking about food to be eaten. I hope also that it has given you food for thought.

11   Veterinary "Problems"

What follows is in no way intended to be a criticism of the veterinary profession. As I only see problem dogs, my findings are unrepresentative of dogs in general, and for every dog I see, there are probably one thousand who are medically treated with no adverse effects on their health or behaviour. But, when it comes to looking at some behavioural problems, veterinary treatment cannot be ruled out as occasionally a cause of those problems.

This is because dogs, like humans, react in different ways to certain drugs. Some people have allergic reactions to tetanus injections or antibiotics, and this is recognised to the point where certain questions are asked before treatment is administered. If the questions are not asked, we are able to volunteer the information based on previous experience before the treatment is administered. This is not so with dogs. With them, we tend to recognise behavioural changes following medical treatment, but not link the two things together. I think that this unfortunately is a direct result of popular opinion and media pressure, which always put dog behaviour problems directly on the shoulders of the owner.

The following case history concerns one of my own dogs. Oliver is a male Weimaraner who, at about two years of age, started to develop an under-belly rash which the vet diagnosed as possibly a grass allergy. Because of the time of year that the problem arose this was quite feasible. He was given an injection of cortisone which was designed to take away the irritation, and it was suggested that, as far as possible, Oliver be kept away from lush-growing grass areas or parks where grass had been newly mown. There is no doubt that as a result of the injection the irritation subsided, but I also noticed that Oliver became more aggressive, not only to other dogs, but also towards people. This was put down to the fact that he was a young adult male dog.

Despite the restrictions on the area in which Oliver could be exercised, after about six weeks the irritation came back, but with it there was a marked reduction in his aggression. Oliver again visited the vet, where he received another injection of cortisone, and the suggestion was made that it might be a contact allergy. As a result, all his bedding was changed and things seemed to settle down, except that Oliver started to become aggressive again towards people and dogs.

It is obvious now that the injection was creating the aggression, but at the time we were more concerned with Oliver's health and did not link his aggression with the injection. As a result, whenever Oliver showed unwanted behaviour patterns, he was punished, either verbally or physically, with a view to teaching him that such behaviour was totally unacceptable. Believe it or not, this whole sequence of events continued for quite a long time before we realised that when Oliver scratched, almost to the point of bleeding, he was quite sociable towards dogs and people. When he did not scratch, he was capable of eating dogs and people. Cortisone is a chemical replacement for the natural hormone Cortisol. It acts as an anti-inflammatory agent and also reduces reactions to allergens.

It took some time for us to realise that the allergic reaction was being caused by his diet. The cortisone was stopping the scratching but increasing the aggression. Once the cortisone wore off, the scatching was resumed and so we were into a vicious circle.

It was not until we started to use a homoeopathic remedy to relieve the irritation that we realised that it could be stopped without creating an aggressive reaction in the dog. We then started to look for root causes and came up with the diet. The diet was eventually changed, the reaction did not occur, there was, therefore, no need for treatment.

Another typical case concerned a ten-year-old Pekingese bitch who had started to fight with a five-year-old Yorkshire Terrier bitch.

They had previously lived in perfect harmony for years. Without doubt the Peke was the aggressor, despite the fact that the Yorkie showed all signs of submission. The situation had deteriorated to the point where the Yorkie spent most of the day hiding in the owner's bedroom, and the owner had plasters on almost every finger of both hands, as a result of trying to break up the fights. It transpired that, over the previous ten weeks leading up to this out-of-character behaviour, the Pekingese had suffered from a variety of medical problems, ranging from ear infections to a rash between the toes. Because of these problems she had been given antibiotics of one type or another. I know that I react to certain antibiotics by getting irritable and suffering from indigestion, and after discussion with the vet, homoeopathic treatment for the dog's medical problems was tried and proved to be successful. Within a few days domestic harmony started to return and the owner reported a 60% improvement. Unfortunately, during the period of aggression, the Peke had learned that she could bully the Yorkie and, as a result, the Yorkie remained terrified. Sometimes separation is the best solution for all concerned and this proved to be the case in this instance. The Peke was found a caring home nearby and settled immediately. The Yorkie has since bounced back to normal.

I have included this case to show that a 100% success rate is not always possible. Without doubt the veterinary treatment was exacerbating the problem and a different approach did produce an improvement, but at the end of the day these two dogs had clearly become incompatible.

Some time ago I wrote a correspondence course for the Canine Studies Institute on man's relationship with dogs. The object of this course from my point of view was to get people who have been working with dogs for many years to realise that there are areas in our relationship which cannot be solved purely by training the dog.

One of the tasks that I set in the work to be completed by the students was this: "From amongst friends or colleagues try to find examples of diet or medical treatment that have affected them, their family members, people they have met, their pets or friends' pets. Report your conclusions, based on what they tell you."

From this I have received a phenomenal amount of information concerning the effects of medical treatments on people. For example, in some of the homes for wayward children, they do not allow coloured toilet paper, because in some cases it has proved to affect the behaviour of the child. If a simple item like that can affect child behaviour then what might we not be doing to our dogs?

I cannot emphasise enough at this point that there is no

substitute for proper veterinary care for your dog. What I am saying is that, if there is an on-going problem that is only being masked by the normal veterinary treatment or if there are side effects to the veterinary treatment that is being received, then there are alternative methods available, of which I feel the reader should be aware. Homoeopathic treatment is available on the National Health; similarly, the fees of a homoeopathic vet are now being covered by the major pet insurance companies. Obviously, you will need your doctor to refer you if you are seeking treatment for yourself and your vet to refer you if you are seeking treatment for your pet.

Alternative, or complementary treatment, can take various forms. One of these was pioneered, many years ago, by Dr Edward Bach, a respected Harley Street physician, who became concerned that hospital beds were being filled up with patients who were ill because of treatment received earlier for some other complaint. I shall be eternally grateful to a lady called Violet Todd who first introduced me to this form of treatment and demonstrated its effect in some remarkable cases.

Dr Bach (pronounced Batch) realised that the increasing use of drugs was only masking the problems and not getting to the root of the causes. His concern resulted in him becoming involved in research into homoeopathic remedies. He realised that without doubt they did work but he was concerned that the average person would find it quite difficult to self-diagnose and, therefore, treat themselves. Dr Bach gave up everything and set out to look for a system of self-help curing that did not have any side effects.

There are now thirty-eight remedies available as a result of Dr Bach's research. These consist simply of the essence of particular naturally occurring substances diluted in water and preserved with a spirit. They are administered in the form of drops from bottles which carry the name of the substance from which they derive. i.e. Larch, Rock Rose, Gorse, Rock Water etc.

Although these "Flower Remedies" are based upon one of the homoeopathic principles – the smaller the dose, the more potent it is – they work on an entirely different plan.

Unlike homoeopathy, the Bach remedies use entirely naturally-occurring substances. Also, unlike homoeopathy, instead of looking at the symptom and finding a remedy, depending on the person or animal type that matches that symptom, Bach remedies ignore the symptom all together and looks only at the character or type of person/animal being treated. The problem that someone who has been "in dogs" for many years is faced with when using the Bach remedies is that you have to look at the dog's behaviour and normal habits as if it were a person. You have to anthropomorphise. (I haven't used a big word for ages and no book about dogs is complete without this word!)

Alternatively, the principle of homoeopathy is to give one or more doses of a highly-diluted substance which in large doses, taken by a healthy person, produces symptoms and signs similar to those from which the patient is suffering.

For example, the homoeopathic tablet derived from the plant Belladonna would be considered in some cases of aggression. The plant itself was first called this by the Italian women who used it to dilate the pupils of their eyes to give them more appeal. One of the classic visible symptoms prior to the onset of aggression is that the pupils dilate.

The word "Homoeopathy" is derived from two Greek words, *"Homoios"* meaning similar and *"Pathos"* meaning disease. The simple explanation of how it is used is: "Let like be treated by like." Working on this principle, I took the view if that Belladonna was good enough for pretty Italian women, it was good enough for my aggressive dogs.

My initial results were fairly mixed. Sometimes my clients reported a remarkable improvement, sometimes no change at all. This was clearly because I was not fully taking into account the *whole* dog. I was making the mistake of categorising a particular remedy to cure a particular problem.

When dealing with any canine behaviour problem it is important to take a holistic approach before the proper behaviour modification or rehabilitation programme can be advised. A holistic approach means that every area that might be affecting the behaviour of the dog is considered. By meeting the family and discussing the entire dog – from where he sleeps, through what he eats, and everything in between – we can ensure that this is done. If, for instance, we do not explore the children's opinions of how they view the dog's role within the family, we might be missing out on a vital area that needs restructuring.

As I became more interested in the homoeopathic approach as an aid to my work, I realised just how important it was to ask questions which were even more searching than the questions that I had asked when trying to discover the root cause of the behaviour problem.

During my initial consultation, I would be asking questions about the dog's early experience: its diet; how it lived within the family structure; formal training experiences; veterinary treatment and so on. In general, from the answers that I received, I could advise the correct rehabilitation programme. As a result of this advice and the back-up facilities that I offer of ongoing telephone advice, most of the behaviour problems that I see are quickly overcome.

If I need to consider a homoeopathic approach when all else has failed, the kind of things I need to know are:

Is the dog hypersensitive to even moderate pain (especially young dogs) and does it react in an aggressive manner? A Chamomilla type.

Does the dog become reluctant and anxious prior to a known event, like entering the dog club or going to the vet, and upon entering becomes aggressive? A Gelsemium type.

Does the aggression relate to some sort of phobia, such as fear of being in a crowded place? An Aconite type.

Does the aggression relate to some sort of phobia (as before), but is usually followed by gastro-intestinal symptoms such as diarrhoea? An Argent Nit. type.

These Homoeopathic remedies all relate to type and that applies not only to dogs, but also to self-diagnosing one's own problems or illnesses. The names of the remedies are probably quite foreign to the majority of readers. Nevertheless, my experience is that they certainly do work. My high regard for this form of treatment is being reinforced all the time.

However, I have to admit that my first experience of the effect that the Bach flower remedies can produce was "mind blowing".

Violet Todd, who I mentioned earlier, is a herbalist who has been using the Bach remedies for over thirty years. I was discussing a particularly resistent case history with her and, based upon what she had been talking about, I asked her whether she thought she could help or not. What follows is a case history which is a tribute, not only to her extraordinary insight, but also to the "power of flower".

Bobby was an eleven-month-old male German Shepherd owned by a very quietly spoken, slightly built Irish girl called Nora. They had been referred to me by their vet, whom Nora had consulted about Bobby's behaviour after she had been unsuccessful at the local dog club. Bobby had tried to attack every dog in the club and would not allow any of the instructors near his owner. Prior to seeing Bobby, I had been told that he was "as big as a house" and very aggressive. This proved to be a perfect description and made me wonder (as I often do) whether we are doing the right thing by trying to rehabilitate dogs like this who appear to be temperamentally unstable and whose behaviour is socially unacceptable. Whilst we are trying to change the behaviour, people are at risk.

Normally, I would spend around two hours with every problem dog. This proved to be impossible in Bobby's case and he had to be returned to the car after ten minutes. Clearly, he had a diet problem. He was underweight, his coat was dull, his skin was in a terrible condition, his eyes were crusty and his activity level was incredible. This was not the reason that he was put back into the car. Every move that I tried to make – crossing my legs, picking up a pen, answering the telephone etc. – resulted in such an aggressive display by Bobby that I began to wonder whether Nora would be able to hang on to him. I advised a diet change and arranged to see them again in two weeks.

During this second appointment, it was evident that the diet had helped physically but his behaviour remained the same. There was no way that I could help Nora to control her dog because Bobby would not let me move at all.

The frightening thing about him was that every sound or movement brought about an excitable aggression which did not subside: the next sound or movement only added to the aggression. After discussing the case with the referring vet, I recommended a course of homoeopathic treatment: Belladonna for the aggression, and Kali Phos for the hypersensitivity to sound. This resulted in a very slight improvement but by this time Bobby was entering full maturity and his confidence in his ability to intimidate people was growing. We were fighting a losing battle and the prospect of euthanasia was on the horizon. The only thing going in Bobby's favour was that at no time had he ever shown the slightest aggression to Nora and he had never actually bitten anybody. It was at this stage that Violet agreed to see him.

During the first appointment he behaved towards Violet in exactly the way that he had behaved towards me in the past and all the notes had to be recorded after he left because neither of us could reach for a pen at the time. (This might sound incredible, but it is true.)

Violet described him in the following way: If Bobby were a man, he would be the type that would be a child molester or a rapist: a person who would seek sexual self-gratification with no regard for the feelings of others. He acted as if he possessed Nora, but showed no love or emotion towards her. Violet suggested remedies for this type of character.

When we next saw Bobby, he had been having treatment for two weeks. Nora allowed him to sniff both of us and then let go of his lead. Violet and I were understandably a little bit nervous, but Nora seemed quite confident. Bobby spent a few minutes sniffing around and then lay down in the middle of the floor and started to doze. The telephone rang and I was able to answer it. Violet got up from her chair, went to the door and pretended to speak to somebody outside. All that Bobby did was to show interest. This amazing transformation was adequately summed up when Violet turned to me and said: "That's the first time I have ever seen you lost for words."

Violet saw Bobby on four more occasions when the remedies were altered slightly according to the information about his behaviour that Nora supplied and our impressions of him at the time. This change in behaviour also gave me the opportunity to advise Nora on how best to control Bobby. The Bach remedies and increased control were working hand in glove with each other. On the last visit, Bobby shook hands with me and gave Violet a kiss.

I must admit to being fairly sceptical at first and slightly reluctant to talk about this form of treatment in dog training circles: I was afraid that it might ruin my "street credibility". Now, I have no hesitation at all because I know that these remedies work. If others do not want to listen, then they are the losers.

When I first started to work at the Woodthorpe Veterinary Group, I was not sure how the vets there would feel about my views on homoeopathy and Bach remedies. I had no need to worry – the group principal, Keith Butt, is interested in the subject and anyway is forward thinking enough to set up a referral behaviour clinic. Richard Bleckman has been using the Bach Flower Remedies for a number of years in conjunction with his usual veterinary skills. It was on the first day of working there that I noticed a dropper bottle of the Bach remedy "Crab Apple". I asked Richard, "Under what circumstances would you use this?" His reply was, "Many, but probably most frequently after an animal has been on a course of antibiotics, I would then use the crab apple to flush the system". I remember thinking "what a brilliant use of complementary medicine, not instead of, but alongside traditional medicine". (Crab apple is a Bach remedy which is known as the "cleanser".)

As you can see, it is a very modern and enlightened practice. I attend on one day a week for three weeks, dealing with canine behaviour problems. On the fourth week, my colleague and a fellow member of the Association of Pet Behaviour Consultants, Peter Neville BSc, advises on feline behaviour problems.

Peter is recognised as this country's foremost expert on feline behaviour and because of his academic training as a biologist, has always had a very scientific approach towards the treatment of behaviour problems: until recently that is. He rang me to ask if I could recommend (in his own words) "one of your homoeopathic drugs", which I thought was an interesting choice of words. The problem was that he had been treating a male cat who lived in a household with many other cats and was being aggressive towards all of them – so much so that the other cats were living in fear of him. As Peter said, the problem could probably be resolved if the owner would allow the cat to go out periodically so that it could receive more mental stimulation and become less territorial.

Apparently, the owner would not do this because of her fear that he would get run over or atttacked by a dog. I suggested that he should try a Bach remedy and I briefly described the type of character that each remedy was aimed at. I started to describe the Vine type: *Dominating/inflexible/tyrannical/arrogant.* Before I could go any further, he said: "Stop there; that's him exactly."

About a week later, I received another call from him which started with, "You're not going to believe this, but that stuff worked. The owner thinks I'm the best thing since sliced bread."

I assured him that I did believe him and also promised not to shatter the owner's rose-tinted view of him. Since then, Peter has tried these remedies on many occasions with similar success. His view is the same as mine: it is important to get the environment and all other influencing factors right first. In most cases, this results in there being no symptom left to treat. If there is, Peter now offers his clients, through the referring vet, a choice between a homoeopathic approach or drug therapy. In almost every case, the owner opts for the homoeopathic approach.

Although I use homoeopathic remedies in certain cases, it is the Bach remedies that I usually opt for.

Because there are only thirty-eight of them, it makes diagnosing a problem much easier. By combining four or five remedies that relate to the character of the dog – one remedy does not interfere with the effect of another – you can usually be assured that one of them does the trick. For example, let us assume that we are dealing with a nervous individual. Perhaps it is a show dog that is not particularly confident in general, but goes to pieces completely in the ring and is getting worse. The following combination might prove successful:

Aspen:	*Apprehension for no known reason*
Cherry Plum:	*Uncontrolled, irrational thoughts*
Larch:	*Lack of self confidence, feels inferior, fears failure*
Mimulus:	*Fear of known things, shyness, timidity*
Rock Rose:	*Suddenly alarmed, scared, panicky.*

Providing one or more of these remedies match the dog's character, then a beneficial effect will be seen very quickly. How dramatic that effect is depends on how long the dog has been suffering from the problem. Normally, a course of between three and six weeks is all that is required and the effects tend to remain.

I never use a homoeopathic or Bach remedy on its own, they are always accompanied by a programme of rehabilitation. For instance, in the case of the nervous show dog, the owners would be advised to set up a show situation, usually at their ring-craft class, but instead of putting the dog through the routine of being examined by the judge, the judge would approach, give a titbit and move on to the next dog. He would approach again later, give a titbit, stroke the dog once, give another titbit and then move on again. Over the weeks, this would be built upon until the dog had the attitude of "Please put me in a show ring with as many judges as possible."

The most unusual case I treated with Bach remedies was a five-year-old crossbred, spayed bitch who became frightened of going into one particular area in the flat in which it lived.

The owner eventually narrowed the problem down to a particular wall within that area, by encouraging and bribing the dog to enter the room and observing how it would shy away from that one wall.

She visited her neighbours to make sure that none of them had installed new hi-fi equipment, or anything that could cause vibration or ultra-sonic sounds that the dog might have detected and which might cause her concern. None was found. In desperation, she called in the local priest who blessed the flat. It made no difference.

The problem increased to the point where the dog became frightened of entering the flat itself; then the block where the flat was situated, and eventually the road leading to the block. Away from the area the dog was perfectly at ease.

The flat is on the third floor of a block that is situated in a quiet private housing complex. The wall that was proving to be the root cause of the dog's escalating fearfulness was opposite a window that looked out over some playing fields. On that wall was a large mirror.

As far as she could recall, the owner was able to pinpoint the start of the problem to be around early November.

In the absence of any other information and assuming that high-frequency sound, strange vibrations, ghouls and ghosts had been eliminated, I did what most behaviourists have to do occasionally: I guessed.

I suggested that perhaps one dark evening when the dog was alone and in that particular room, a rocket had exploded outside the window causing a flash to appear in the mirror on the wall. (For early November, this was a reasonable assumption.) Upon her return, she may have recognised increased signs of anxiety in her dog and paid more attention to her than she would normally have done.

As the days progressed, she probably compounded the problem by trying to reassure her dog that there was nothing to worry about, thus rewarding the unwanted behaviour. Having finally recognised that the problem was the wall, she convinced the dog that there was something strange about it by feeling it, listening to it and callling strangers in to splash things on it.

I advised the following treatment:

1. The owner had to be offhand, even slightly intolerant, whenever her dog started to show the first signs of fear. She was told not to be cross with her dog, just to make sure that she did not reward the behaviour by showing sympathy.
2. The curtains were drawn across the offending window and the mirror was temporarily removed to avoid any reflection from car headlights etc.
3. The dog's feeding place was moved from the kitchen to that room and the bowl placed gradually nearer to the wall.
4. Three times a day she was given four drops of Dr Bach's remedies: Aspen, Mimulus and Rock Rose.

Which one of these four steps had the greater effect, we do not know. On this occasion, it was the result that was important. The dog made a complete recovery.

Probably, the most satisfying case which involved the use of a homoeopathic remedy was the first case that I tried it on. My introduction to this form of treatment – and subsequently the Bach remedies – was through what Richard Allport MRCVS (honorary veterinary advisor to the APBC) calls the TEETH principle: Tried Everything Else, Try Homoeopathy.

The case concerned a Dobermann bitch that had been obtained from a rescue society at fourteen months of age. My client, a single woman in her early twenties and living on her own, worked just a few doors away from where she lived and was able to get back to her dog regularly throughout the day. The problem was that whenever she left the dog, it either became destructive, defecated or urinated. The longest time the dog was ever left was two to three hours.

I advised a programme that was designed to relieve the anxiety that was clearly being caused by an over-attachment to the new owner. (Attachment/Anxiety is covered in more detail in Chapter 15.) I was surprised to hear that the improvement had only been minor. Under the circumstances, I would have expected a complete cure. I had no doubt that my client had understood why her dog was behaving in the way that it was, nor did I doubt that she was doing everything that I had told her to do.

After a quick chat with her vet, we decided to try *Ignatia*, a homoeopathic remedy in tablet form used for people who are depressed or have suffered a bereavement – also useful for dogs and cats which pine when they are left in boarding kennels. A complete cure was achieved within twenty-four hours.

In summary, I only use a homoeopathic or Bach approach after every other area has been investigated. I always seek the referring vet's approval before doing so and I always use them in conjunction with a behaviour modification programme. The increased success rate that I have enjoyed since I included this form of therapy in my arsenal of weapons for curing behaviour problems makes me think that perhaps we are just scratching the surface of the avenues that are available to us, provided we are prepared to keep an open mind.

12   Training "Problems" for Trainers

So far, I have touched upon the areas that are not generally considered when it comes to trying to work out why a dog does what it does. Nevertheless, my case notes show that all of them should be considered before a course of action is decided upon. Now let us look at another cause of bad behaviour – certain traditionally-accepted training methods and the application of old wives' tales.

We have already discussed the way dogs relate to the "rub their nose in the mess that they have made" theory and what the dog actually learns from this. What has convinced people in the past that this has worked has been the fact that dogs have eventually stopped soiling indoors and have learnt to ask to go out. The fact that this would have happened naturally is never considered.

We assume that the method has worked and we do not see that we have created mistrust about our intentions when we enter the room. With the more submissive type of dog, our entry into the room results in a wriggly, cringing approach that in dog terms is designed to signify: "I recognise your superior status and I am just a worm." A canine way of exhibiting submission is to urinate. We see the dog do this and freak out. A vicious circle has been created: the dog displays normal canine submission and, working on the old wives' principle, we punish it. It is important to remember that a £2000 Persian carpet is just the floor of a den to a dog.

Punishment just does not work as an aid to teaching any species of animal anything. We recognise that if we call the cat and it runs off, there is nothing that we can do about it other than to find some method that will encourage it to respond to our call. If the same thing happens when we call the dog, we get annoyed and want to punish it.

Revenge is an emotion that is peculiar to humans – revenge, that is, in the context of punishment after the act, as opposed to instant retribution. I recently watched two young girls trying to catch a pony in a field. After five minutes they gave up and went to get a feed for it. When they returned and shook the food bowl the pony approached very cautiously. They put a head collar on it and then hit it across the neck three times with a riding crop. Their comment was that it had to be taught a lesson. They could not grasp the principle that all they had probably taught the pony was not to approach them, even if food was involved.

I am sure that they were not in any way sadistic but that their attitude was learned from people whom they regarded as experts within the horse world. They genuinely thought that they were doing the right thing.

How many times do you see people hitting their dog when they eventually catch it in an attempt to teach it not to run away in the future? Luckily, things are beginning to change in both worlds, and I was interested to read a report recently about an American horse-trainer who uses a radically new method of what he calls, "starting" young, unbroken horses, the process that we have always known as "breaking".

His name is Monty Roberts and he has degrees in biological science, agri-economics and animal behaviour. He has a fervent belief that the old ways of breaking horses are wrong. With the comment "there ain't gonna be no pain", he goes on to explain that he would very much like to create a better world for the horse than the one it currently finds. That is a comment which could equally be applied to dogs, especially in the view of the strong anti-dog lobby that is prevalent at this time.

He uses a method of "advance and retreat" based upon the horse's natural patterns of including a stranger within the herd. The idea is to create an understanding, based upon herd instinct, of the role of each member in the herd.

What Monty Roberts has done is to reject the old ideas of how horses should be broken. In his own words he says: "Does a teacher suddenly grab a child by its hair, give it a shaking and beat it on its first day at school? The day a horse is broken is the most traumatic in its life. It gets jabbed in the mouth and kicked in the ribs just to be told who is the boss. We have not changed our methods since before Christ." His method does not involve hitting, jerking, pulling, tying or restraining. The basic premise is simple: there is an unwritten contract between the unstarted horse and man. If the unfettered equine is prepared to be with the handler – "joined up" – and follow him/her around like a dog at heel, then life is good in the "comfort zone", a position close to the trainer. If not, the horse has to be sent away to trot or to canter. Horses usually leave the handler an average of three times before "joining up".

One of the comments that I received from an observer was, "It worked like magic, but not the sort of magic you press a button for. It takes account of the horse's psychology." What magic are they talking about? It is that, by using this technique, young horses can be ridden for the first time, within thirty minutes on average, without stress, force or trauma.

Monty's message has since been taken up by some horsemen in Canada, Argentina, British Columbia and India. Here in Britain he has "started" twenty-one of the Queen's horses, as well as dozens of volunteered horses, most of which, I am sure, were put forward with the attitude that "This one will prove the method does not work". He has even been contacted by school authorities and psychologists for advice on dealing with problem teenagers who are addicts, kleptomaniacs and truants. If you think back to the earlier chapter about the dog in the human pack, you will see that Monty Roberts' principles are much the same: first establish a leader role and then lay down the rules. The only way to go forward, I believe, is to listen to a man like Monty Roberts, to witness the results that he gets, or at least to think about the sense behind what he is teaching. The time has come for a change.

So let us look at the way that dogs today are traditionally trained. Firstly, most people regard dog training as a mechanical process which requires enrolling at a local club so that they can teach their dog how to behave.

Pet owners taking their dogs to training classes is a relatively new thing. Twenty or thirty years ago, dog clubs were mainly attended by dog-obedience people interested primarily in competitions. They have always offered help and advice to pet owners but, obviously, this advice was influenced by the precision of their sport. That meant that the dog must always sit straight; it must hold a dumb-bell without chewing it etc. Of course, being able to teach your dog to perform on command to this high level is a mark of your control within an exercise situation but it is not relevant to the needs of the average pet owner.

The increased popularity of dog clubs has stemmed from:
1. More public awareness of owner responsibility.
2. An increasing anti-dog lobby.
3. TV dog training programmes.
4. More free time available to the owners.
5. More problems arising as a result of our lifestyle.

Without doubt more people are attending classes and this should be a good thing. However, the sport of dog obedience has altered very little over the years, and the training given in general has not changed. My advice to owners is always to go and watch without your dog. If you do not like what you see, the chances are that neither will your dog. There is a growing army of forward-thinking training clubs, and it is up to the owner to be selective in their choice.

Secondly, many dog clubs do not interview their students about the behaviour of the dog within the home environment. As a result, they give advice on how the dog should be trained within a false environment where the dog eventually realises that it has no other option than to do as it is told. Alternatively, the owners with a dog that objects in an aggressive manner to what it regards as an infringement upon the established pecking order are quite often made to feel unwelcome, or openly asked to leave because their dog is disrupting the rest of the class. I know that this is true because the majority of my clients tell me so.

I admit that this comment is biased because these are the dogs that are eventually referred to me. I do not see the dogs who successfully complete their training and whose numbers greatly exceed the drop-out rate. I can also recognise the problems that trainers are faced with when a disruptive, aggressive dog joins a class. They have to consider the class as a whole, not only from the safety angle, but also from the point of view that one problem dog in a class of fifteen will result in fourteen of them learning nothing.

Thirdly, the majority of classes are started with a heelwork exercise. There seems to be some kind of unwritten law that everyone should walk in a clockwise circle, with the dogs on their owners' left. From the dog's point of view, this allows all of the dogs to herd all of the humans. The result is that tails go up into a dominant position, the noise level increases as a verbal expression of attitude, and the pulling gets worse because a dog that herds the pack must have the right to lead the pack. On the other hand if you walk just slightly faster than a slow pace in an anti-clockwise direction, the tail carriage starts to droop and the noise level subsides. The result of this is that the dogs become easier to control because the humans have taken on the role of herders because the dogs are on the inside.

What follows are some suggestions which have proved success-ful in the past, and which might help club instructors to overcome some of the problems that they are regularly faced with. They should also help to increase their success rate.

1. Never allow a first-time instructor to take the beginner class. They may have proved themselves to be excellent at training a dog, but teaching other people is an art on its own. The skills involved rarely come naturally. They have to be learned. Allow them to assist a qualified or experienced instructor, or let them try their hand at the second and more advanced class (under supervision). All too often I find the first class under the supervision of the most junior teacher and this is the class that needs, and expects, the most experienced, competent and knowledgeable advice.
2. Always start each member of a beginner group on the same day. The practice of having flexible lessons where new members are allowed to join at any time is unfair on the whole class – unfair and embarrassing for the new student and definitely unfair on the new dog. A new student needs extra attention, and with only one instructor on the floor, this must be to the detriment of the time allocated to the rest of the group. Even if an assistant is allocated to advise the new student, the student often gets the feeling that the rest of the group is watching.

   The most important consideration should be given to the dog. Within a very short space of time, dogs that attend on a regular basis form themselves into almost a feral pack. They might not have the tight structure of the domestic pack but nevertheless they become familiar with each other and a kind of pecking order is established. Any newcomer becomes an intruder and a great deal of posturing takes place. The newcomer knows that it is trespassing into an area where there is already an established group and will feel very insecure. An insecure dog cannot learn.

3. Prior to starting any new group, find out whether any of the dogs have aggressive tendencies towards other dogs. If so, it is a good idea to ask the owner to leave the dog in the car until the rest of the class has settled down and the dogs feel comfortable in each other's presence. At the start of any new class, each dog thinks that *it* is the trespasser and so very rarely is there any trouble. Once a relaxed atmosphere has been reached the macho dog can be bought in. This dog will feel the air of acceptance among the dogs present and will be subdued by this. Regardless of breed, size or genetic status, all dogs are aware of the trespass laws and this is why the smallest and least aggressive of dogs will chase other dogs off its property. This simple procedure allows you to integrate a new group with little or no trouble.

The owners of the dog will be more than happy to comply because their dog's aggression is probably the reason why they enrolled in the first place. By showing them that the aggression can be contained, you will give them the incentive to keep coming. If you explain what is going to happen, the rest of the group will find the insight into canine behaviour fascinating, and this will start to make them realise that there is more to training dogs than pushing a button here or pulling a lever there.

4. Never start a new class off with heelwork. Noise and rapid movement will increase excitement and heighten the risk of aggressive confrontations. It should be the aim of any instructor to establish a calm environment in which to train both dogs and owners. Static exercises like the "Sit" or "Down" will help you to achieve this quickly. Sitting everyone down in a large circle on the floor (or mats if your club is posh) with the dogs held on a lead but not being told to do anything specific, will result quite quickly in most of the dogs lying calmly next to their owners, or just sitting if they prefer.

Whilst you are waiting for calmness to prevail, you can discuss the aims of training and what they can all expect to get out of the sessions in the weeks to come. It helps to explain exactly why the lesson is being started this way. Once the owners grasp the principle that the environment is important to the learning process, they will not expect a fully-trained dog as a result of just one lesson. During this time, diet can be discussed, or equipment, or even the importance of the pack structure at home. A properly structured first lesson which avoids movement exercises is the key to a successful course.

5. If over the period of the following weeks, one of the dogs starts to become disruptive, especially in terms of aggression to other dogs, steer clear of punishment. The object of any training exercise is to teach the dog to behave in an acceptable manner at all times, not just when there is fear of retribution. The only thing a dog might learn from this sort of technique is not to show aggression in the dog club when wearing a lead and choke chain. This is training through fear, and if the dog is fearful of the owner's action, its ability to learn other things will be impaired. What the dog *will* learn is that the presence of another dog is a prelude to punishment, so it is good canine insurance to chase that other dog off before the owner sees it. In other words, punishment can heighten a problem and generally does.

One way of curbing canine aggression within a club environment is to revert to the pack herding instinct. (It is important to note that the following procedure should only be used under supervision.) Place the handler and the dog in the middle of the floor, dog on leash, which should be attached to an ordinary buckle collar. This is important, because the object of the exercise is not to punish, merely to restrain. Any pain-associated aggression should be avoided. The dog should not be put in any formal position. Form a circle of handlers and dogs around them at a distance that will avoid contact if the dog in the middle lunged outward at the same time that a dog lunged inward. Four or five dogs are usually sufficient and these should be carefully selected. Overly-submissive or dominant characters should not be included.

Start the circle moving at a slow pace in an anti-clockwise direction. This enables the handlers to herd their dogs, which in turn are herding the dog in the centre. Initially, the dog will fly out at one or more of the herding dogs and might receive a similar response. All aggression should be checked on both sides, but no words of command used either negative or positive. After a few minutes, the dog in the middle will become quieter and the tail carriage will start to fall. At this point, the outside circle can close in a little bit. After a few more circles, you will notice that the dog in the middle will refuse to make eye contact with any of the dogs on the outside. When this situation has been reached, the circle can be broken and the dog taken out of the room for about ten minutes.

If this exercise is repeated again, the dog in the middle might make a token attempt at aggression, but this will not last long and should be treated in just the same way as earlier. As the circle closes in slightly, you will see slight signs of submission from the dog in the middle. Break off again and repeat the exercise in about ten minutes time. This time the dog will make every effort to get out of the circle: the job has been completed and the aggressive dog has been subdued by the pack. This usually has a long-term effect within that environment and a knock-on effect towards dogs outside the environment. Care should be taken not to overdo the herding, and the technique should only be used after every other avenue has been tried and failed, i.e. diet, environmental pack restructuring, medical attention etc.

6. Recognise the fact that some dogs do not respond to training within a club environment. You should be constantly looking for signs of stress amongst the dogs in your class. Some dogs might exhibit stress reactions to certain exercises. This can usually be alleviated by changing the method used. With some dogs, just being in a class can be stressful. If this is the case, they will never learn anything and a good instructor will point out the symptoms to the owner, and should be able to offer advice or help with either outdoor classes or private tuition. Unfortunately, a lot of trainers refuse to recognise that their training classes do not suit all dogs and persevere regardless, usually laying the faults in the dog squarely on the shoulders of the owner. As a result, many dogs are being forced into stressful situations, and instead of helping the owners to cope with these dogs, the instructors are actually creating problems that the dogs did not have prior to joining the club.

Many of my clients have told me that on the second or third visit to the dog club, their dog refused to go in.

Invariably, the advice was to make the dog obey. Whether these dogs were being bloody-minded or in a total state of panic is immaterial. The fact that they did not want to return for more lessons should be telling someone something.

13   "Problems" with the Pack

The following chapter is all about actual case histories and how they were resolved. It looks at the problems with dogs and babies; dogs and children; dogs and adults; and dogs and dogs. During this chapter, I shall be stretching the "Think Dog" concept to its ultimate limit, because I shall be advising a reward-based approach towards what some people will regard as totally unacceptable behaviour.

To suggest that if the dog growls you should give it a titbit will make the majority of dyed-in-the-wool dog trainers throw up their hands in horror. They will obviously take the view that you are praising the wrong behaviour. Yet, if you really understand dogs, you will realise that, provided you have taken into account all of the areas that might affect behaviour and are confident that you have got all of this right, then the only reason why dogs will bark, growl at you or bite is because they do not trust you. The "Think Dog" approach is designed to calm the dog's fears of what the human intends to do.

It should also be understood that for the majority of my clients, I am the last but one resort. They are usually resigned to the fact that if what I advise does not work they will have to have the dog put down. Before reaching me, they have usually sought advice from a variety of different sources and almost always the confrontational, "show it who's the boss" methods have been tried and failed. Quite often, the problem has been exacerbated by following this advice. It is my job to match the dog with the family and this usually involves a complete reversal of how their lifestyle together has evolved. Food is used extensively, because it works; and, if you carefully consider the procedures outlined, you will realise just why it works.

DOGS AND BABIES

Dear Mr Fisher,
My four-year-old West Highland Terrier, Ben, has started to become
aggressive to my eleven-month-old son, Jason. They have always got on so

well together. Since Jason started to crawl (about two months ago), Ben has tended to avoid him a bit, but he has never before shown him the slightest aggression. For the past week or so, the whole family has been ill with flu. Luckily neither Jason or our live-in Nanny caught it. So to be safe, Nanny has been caring for Jason more than usual.

Yesterday, I began to feel a bit better and so Nanny let Jason come to see me. As he crawled through my bedroom doorway, Ben stood up on my bed and started to growl at him quite fiercely. I told him off and my husband smacked him and shut him in the kitchen. He knew that he had done wrong because he was quite subdued for the rest of the day. That evening, whilst my husband was preparing Ben's dinner, Jason crawled into the kitchen. For no reason at all, Ben flew at him and bit his face. Luckily, the damage was not too severe, just a tooth mark under the right eye and another one on his top lip. He was more frightened than hurt, I think.

We don't want to have Ben put to sleep, but we are frightened that it might happen again. Please can you help? We are obviously not allowing Jason to go anywhere near Ben at the moment, but we cannot carry on like this. – Mrs J., Bolton, Lancs.

Whenever the reported problem involves aggression towards children, I always ask the owners if they are certain that they want to keep the dog. Most of these cases can be resolved successfully, but until each has been, the risk of serious damage being done is always present, to say nothing of the psychological effect it might be having on the child. In this particular case, they decided to give Ben another chance. Although I was pretty certain what the cause and the cure were, to be safe I advised the owners to ask their vet to give Ben a check over. (It is surprising how many times impacted anal glands or ear infections can change a dog's behaviour, or for that matter any other underlying and brewing medical problem.) He was given a clean bill of health and the vet referred the case back to me.

It was obvious in this case that the warning signs had been misread. The fact that since Jason had started to crawl, Ben had chosen to stay out of his way shows that Ben had started to view their relationship in a different way. Perhaps he no longer felt confident around Jason or, more likely, had started to view Jason's increased mobility as a threat to him. Warning bells should have been ringing at this point, but I can understand how easy it was to miss the signs when you have grown to trust the dog with the baby.

What had tipped the balance, from the dog avoiding the baby to a clear warning by the dog for the baby to stay away, was the change in the domestic routine as a result of illness, in particular the illness of Jason's mother. This had resulted in a number of days when Mum paid less attention to Jason and more attention to Ben by virtue of the fact that he spent the majority of his time curled up on her bed.

This had effectively raised Ben's status over Jason's and possibly even over Jason's parents. Chapter 3 explains how easily this can happen if we are not aware of the danger. The simple act of Jason entering what Ben had come to consider one of his sleeping areas had resulted in the warning growl. The fact that he had been punished for displaying perfectly normal (albeit unacceptable) behaviour had confused Ben. His display of guilt was not guilt at all; he was merely responding to the air of gloom and concern.

The nature of the injury that Ben inflicted upon Jason when his food was being prepared indicated that the attack was meant as a disciplinary measure. It was not in fact a bite, the jaw muscles were not used to close the mouth. It was a clear-cut canine warning: "Stay away from my food." This is how a higher-ranking dog would warn off a lower-ranking dog. The trouble is that human skin splits more easily than canine skin. The question should be asked: "What right did the dog think that it had to discipline the offspring of what should be the Alpha pair?"

So the real facts of this case were that when Jason started to crawl Ben avoided him, thus giving him freedom to move about. Ben was not particularly happy about it, but he clearly saw that he had no right to stop it. By granting him extra privileges and giving him more attention, whilst at the same time isolating Jason, as Ben saw it, his owners raised Ben's status and lowered Jason's.

So far as Ben was concerned, he had a perfect right to display aggression as a form of discipline. This, if you think about it, is different to being aggressive. A controlled reversal of the roles stopped any further problems arising.

Dear Mr Fisher,
We have tried to introduce our three-year-old Boxer, Bruno, to our new baby, he gets so excited that he jumps up and claws at him. We have read that you should put the baby on the floor and let the dog investigate it,

without letting it lick the face, but we are frightened that Bruno will cause
some damage.

   He is not at all aggressive, but he has always used his claws to rip open
bags when I have been shopping etc. I have never stopped him doing this.

   In fact I always make sure that the bag that he can rip open is the one
that has his bone in it. I am sure that Bruno thinks that there is something
else wrapped up with the baby that is for him. I make him sit, but as soon
as I say, "Look Bruno, it's your new brother", he jumps up and starts
clawing. What am I going to do? – Mrs H., Enfield, London.

This was obviously a straightforward case of learned behaviour.
In this particular instance, I visited the home not just to help
with the introduction, but to assess whether there was an element
of aggression in the dog's attempts to paw at the baby. There
was not.

What usually happened when the mother returned from a
shopping expedition was that she would make sure that all the
other bags were out of harm's way, during which time Bruno
would sit. When only that bag that contained his bone was
available to him she would say to him, "Look what's in here
Bruno", which caused Bruno to attack the bag with his claws
until he got to the bone. When we teach our dogs these silly little
tricks, we never consider the possible consequences. Holding a
little bundle and making Bruno sit was all a prelude to him
reacting to the trigger word "Look". All we needed to teach
Bruno was that there was nothing wrapped up with the baby for
him.

Apparently, Bruno would sell his soul for a piece of white
chocolate. Although I doubt that your average feral dog or wolf
cousin would include this on its hunting list, if it was what Bruno
liked, I decided to use it. Mum sat down holding the baby, and
on the table next to her she had three or four pieces of chocolate.
Bruno was allowed in and went straight over to her. She told
him to sit, which he did with a look of anticipation on his face.
Without saying anything, she gave him a piece of chocolate from
the table. He was then ignored for about thirty seconds whilst
we spoke together and then was given another piece. By this
time, Bruno was completely ignoring the baby and the table was
holding his concentration. We followed this procedure until all
the chocolate had gone. I instructed Mum to tell him what she
usually does to denote that it had all gone. Bruno looked

resigned, sniffed the baby briefly and lay down next to her. The excitement had been satisfied.

She followed this routine over the next three or four occasions, and Bruno quickly learnt that the presence of the baby was a prelude to reward, but not one that was wrapped up with the baby. I was amused to hear that on the day following my visit her mother-in-law arrived, and was extremely concerned by the way that Bruno sat next to the baby and drooled.

I have used this as an example to show that bringing a new baby into a house where there is already a well-established resident dog is not always as straightforward as one would imagine. Providing the temperament of the dog towards the owners is right, the dog will normally accept the new addition to the pack. I always advise my clients to make sure that they do not isolate their dogs when feeding, bathing and changing the baby, but to include it by also talking to the dog occasionally. If the new parents are concerned at all, it is a good idea to use a principle similar to the one we used for Bruno. Give the dog a rawhide chew stick in the same room as they are doing whatever they are doing with the baby, and make sure that this is the only time it gets one of these treats. The dog will soon begin to regard the baby as something nice to be around.

Not many parents would leave a baby alone with their dog, regardless of the dog's temperament. I do stress this point, however, especially if the baby is wearing a dirty nappy. A dog's values are different from ours, and a dirty nappy is a thing to be investigated. Jumping up to investigate a smell from a carry cot or pram can have all sorts of drastic consequences. Tipped over cots and prams usually lead to crying babies, frightened dogs, irate owners and false accusations that the dog tried to drag the baby from the pram. Result: dead dogs.

The most bizarre case I have ever had concerned a baby. It involved a two-year-old male Boxer called Sam. He lived with his mistress and her young baby in Service accommodation. Her husband was in the Navy and away for a lot of the time, and the reported problem was that on his last visit home, the dog had growled at him on three or four occasions. The man was basically frightened of dogs and they had bought Sam as a pup to help him overcome his fear. Because of this, when the dog growled, it was his mistress that punished him. It horrified me to hear that her method of punishment was to bite Sam's ear. Not that I felt particularly sorry for the dog, but I know that I would not put my face down to any growling dog. Her husband's parting words as he left to rejoin his ship were: "Get the dog cured, or get rid of it."

On the face of it, it seemed to be a straightforward case of dominance aggression. The age of the dog, the fact that in the master's absence he became the ranking male, and the amount and length of time his master was away, all pointed towards this being the cause of the problem. Under these circumstances, it is not unusual for the dog to challenge the master for leadership upon his return.

I advised a programme that was designed to reduce the dog's rank in the eyes of his mistress, with instructions on what her husband should do on his next visit home. As the level of control that she had over the dog in general was very good, I assumed that it was obviously just an attitude and not a training problem.

I received a phone call some weeks later to say that her husband was home and the dog was terrifying him; so much so that one day, when she was out shopping, he had shut himself in the kitchen until she came home. He was adamant that the dog had to be put down. They both agreed to come and see me this time, and, naturally, they brought the baby.

We were about half an hour into the consultation and I was becoming more and more confused as to why Sam was not responding to the programme that I had advised. According to the answers that I was receiving, the owners were doing every-thing right. Perhaps, under the circumstances, a complete cure was a lot to ask for but the problem should have started to get better, not worse.

At this point, the baby started to cry and Sam became very agitated to the point where he started to climb on his mistress. Her husband made a move to get up, presumably to call Sam off, but he sat down very quickly when Sam told him to. I must admit I would have done too. Sam clearly meant, "Sit down."

His wife managed to control Sam but he was still very agitated over the baby crying; we put him in the car so that we could carry on our conversation without her husband being afraid of moving. She explained that the reason why Sam had changed at that point was because the baby was breast fed and Sam had to be shut out of the room at feeding time.

I asked if it was normal to shut the dog away at feeding times. (This is something that I always advise people not to do when a new baby is introduced into a house where there is already a resident dog, because it can create problems if the dog learns that it will be isolated whenever the mother wants to pay attention to the baby: feeding, bathing, nappy changing etc.)

"Yes, I have to, otherwise he tries to push the baby out of the way," she said.

"Why should he do that?" I asked innocently.

"Because I have an excess of milk, the midwife said that if I give it to the dog, it will help to form a bond between him and the baby."

Before any new mothers who might be reading this rush off to feed the dog, let me assure you that it will have no effect on the relationship between your dog and your baby. I have no doubt that the midwife meant that she should express the excess milk, prior to giving it to the dog. Sam's mistress had obviously not understood it in this way.

The thought of someone breast feeding an adult male Boxer still makes me shudder, but it did answer a lot of questions. There is nothing in the canine code designed to promote rank better than managing to be first to the most lucrative teat.

DOGS AND CHILDREN

It is not unusual when I am dealing with a case of (so called) hyperactive behaviour in a dog to find that the children are also hyperactive. There is no doubt that the environment in which a dog lives has a tremendous effect upon its behaviour.

If you take two puppies from the same litter and place one with an elderly, very quiet couple, the result is usually a quiet, well-mannered dog. Put the other one into a family environment with two or three active, noisy children and the result will be a dog that acts in the same way.

It is very "Green" to blame food additives, preservatives, colourings etc. for the hyperactive behaviour of children. In some cases, I have no doubt that they do indeed have an effect, as they must do with some dogs. I take the view, however, that if there is some chemical influence, then the child or dog will be uncontrollable until that influence is removed. I see too many cases of reported hyperactivity in a dog from families who bring along (so called) hyperactive children.

One of my cases involved an eighteen-month-old, castrated Springer Spaniel. He had been castrated because the owners had been advised that this would calm him down. This is quite likely to be the case where the problem is hormone related, and I am fully in favour of neutering both dogs and bitches especially if it can be established that the root cause is hormone imbalance. In this particular case, it was not.

From the outset, the dog paced backwards and forwards, jumped on the furniture, scratched at the door and in general acted in a pretty obnoxious manner, but then so did the eight-year-old boy that accompanied them. His name was Adam and within three minutes of being in my office, he interrupted the conversation with the words, "I want to go home, Dad." Dad replied. "Won't be long, Adam."

This continued for quite a long time, even though I dropped subtle hints that I was finding it awfully difficult to continue an investigative conversation whilst being constantly interrupted. Mum muttered something about him being hyperactive but that they had not been able to find the cause yet. Throughout this time, Adam's demands were appeased. He was given books off my shelves without my permission. He was told: "Listen, Adam, this nice man is trying to stop doggie being naughty." He was asked if he wanted to go and see our horses, to which he replied, "No, I want to go home." I was quite grateful for this reply because I had not been asked if he could, and, anyway, I quite like our horses and did not see why Adam should be inflicted upon them.

Throughout this period, my wife was working in the next room. She told me later that, because she could hear what was going on, she had formed the opinion that the boy was retarded. She could not believe it when she learned later that he was not.

After approximately forty minutes of this attention-seeking behaviour, it became quite clear to me that neither Mum nor Dad was going to do anything about it; so I decided to intervene. I waited for the next, "I want to go home," then said, "Adam, do you really want to go home?" He replied, "Yes." So I opened the door and said, "Off you go then. Your Mum and Dad cannot come with you yet, because we have not decided what to do about your dog, but you can go if you want."

Adam looked horror-struck and Mum and Dad gave sheepish grins. He transferred his attentions to Mum by sitting on her knee and putting his "very upset" head on her chest, but he never interrupted again. I had just overcome the effects of additives, preservatives and so on.

The dog looked almost grateful and within minutes became just as calm. I had taken away the stimuli that were making him and me feel like coiled springs.

I have no problem in explaining to owners how to control their dogs' behaviour, but I do not presume to tell them how to control their children, other than to stress the importance of the environmental influence and hope that they pick up on the point. Sadly some do not.

Dear Mr Fisher,
My two children aged eight years and ten years cannot have their friends round to play because our ten-month-old Border Collie bitch follows them everywhere and will nip them if they start running about. She is not an aggressive dog in general, but she just seems to get over-excited when there is a lot of activity. Can you suggest a way to stop her? – Mrs F., Huntington, York.

The herding instinct of the Collie is renowned and this is just what the dog is doing in this particular case. The problem generally stems from the fact that these dogs do not receive enough mental stimulation. They have been bred to work, but because of their popularity as a breed more and more of them are going into domestic environments, probably only getting one or two brief walks a day. As a result they become very pent up and start looking for an outlet for their natural instincts. Put a group of children in front of them with their rapid movements and high-pitched voices and these dogs are in their seventh heaven. Children are even more stimulating than a herd of sheep who tend to stick together most of the time and just need moving around a bit. Children scatter in all directions and it takes a really satisfying effort to control them.

Mrs F. is right. They are generally not aggressive dogs, but any contact with the teeth upon a human must be classified as a bite and is totally unacceptable. When you have a dog like this, the owners must recognise the breed specific needs and ensure that they are catered for. Just walking them is not enough, they need to do things on the walk to exercise their brains as well as their muscles. Chapter 16 is aimed at just this sort of problem.

Because the behaviour is governed by instinct, punishing the dog rarely proves to be a successful solution. You might reach a situation where the dog is frightened of herding the kids when you are present, but you will not take away the urge. What you really need to do is to get the dog to feel comfortable around the children. Getting them to greet the dog calmly and offering a titbit when they first arrive will help to change the dog's expectations about what a group of children is all about. Even getting them to organise a supervised quiet game of "hunt the titbit", will give the dog an outlet for her working abilities. Then put the dog away so that the children can enjoy their other games. When things quieten down and before the children go home, allow her out again for some more calm and rewarding exposure. This sort of regime will probably defuse the situation; and as the children get older and calmer, so will your dog.

Advice based primarily on avoiding the problem might seem strange coming as it does from someone whom people expect to offer a cure for their problem, but I deliberately included this particular situation to make the following points:

1. If you want a lap dog, don't get a Great Dane!
2. If you want a quiet dog, do not get one of the guarding breeds!
3. If you want a dog that does not herd, don't get a Collie!
4. Above all, whatever the problem is, if children are involved, do not take chances!

DOGS AND ADULTS

The voice at the other end of the phone said, "I just went to take his food away and he bit me."

I suppressed the urge to comment that if you did not want the dog to have the food, you should not have given it to him in the first place. Instead I asked what the circumstances were.

Apparently, the owner's wife was expecting a baby and they thought it would be a good idea to teach their dog that they could take its food away when it was eating, in anticipation of the day that the baby might crawl towards the bowl. In principle, it was a very caring idea, and goes to show how much thought some people put in to introducing a baby to a dog. I have put it in that order because almost invariably the dog becomes resident before the baby arrives. (I wonder whether there is some Freudian reason for this – child substitute, perhaps?)

On day one, there was no problem. The dog wagged its tail and looked up expectantly. The same happened on day two and three. On day four, the owner noticed that as he approached the dog went perfectly still with his head still in the bowl. He assumed that the dog knew what was going to happen and had stopped eating so that he could take the bowl away. He did so, the dog did nothing. He was surprised therefore that on day five the dog gave a low growl when he bent down to take the bowl. He smacked the dog for growling and took the bowl away. On this occasion, he did not give him it back for five minutes in order to teach him not to growl in future. On day six, the growl got louder so he smacked him harder and threw his food in the bin as a further punishment. On day seven, the dog bit him as he reached for the food.

With the best of possible motives, this guy had taught his dog to be an aggressive food guarder.

If we look at the circumstances from a "Think Dog" approach, we can begin to understand exactly what has happened. There is a critical area around the dog's mouth that can be best described as the forbidden zone. Anything inside that area belongs to the dog. The modern, domestic, well-fed dog does not usually exhibit this primitive behaviour. Indeed, many of my clients tell me that their dog has a superb temperament because they can take anything out of its mouth with no problem at all. My usual response is: "Do not feed the dog for a week and then try to take a bone away from it." Basic instinct will take over, regardless of breed.

Even in the wild, the most submissive character will defend its food against the most dominant character. The chance of this defence being successful is minimal. If it is successful, the dog will usually exhibit complete submission towards the challenger later, almost as a form of apology. If the rank structure is such that the possessor is very low ranking and the challenger is very high ranking, the challenger would only persevere and win if he were really hungry. A lower rank would not even dream of challenging a higher rank, regardless of hunger pangs.

What this goes to show is exactly how important the law of possession is in canine society. It also shows how biddable most of our domestic dogs have become because we feed them regularly.

If we consider the reported circumstances of this case, we can see that initially the well-fed, always unchallenged dog accepted the removal of its food. Eventually, it got fed up and adopted a classic motionless stance to the approach of another towards its trophy. This is a clear canine warning to stay away which was misread by the owner and subsequently ignored.

As this did not work, the dog escalated the warning and growled. The owner took the view that "No dog is going to growl at me", and hit the dog. We now have a situation where not only is there a challenge for the food, but the challenge is going to be aggressive. How do dogs exhibit aggression? Simple: they bite!

Once he had understood exactly what had happened and why he had been bitten, an alternative programme was relatively easy to introduce. I suggested the following:

1. Change the feeding pattern from once to twice a day: the same daily amount but fed over two meals.
2. Change the food bowl and place of eating so that there is no visual or environmental stimuli that might trigger off mistrust.
3. Buy two similar feeding dishes, and, for the next three or four meals, prepare the dog's food in its presence and place the empty bowl on the floor. (This is quite funny to watch. The dog dives in and then looks up in surprise, then it looks down again, then around the outside, then it tries to look under before looking back up with an expression which says "There's nothing in it, stupid." You take the view, "Oh, silly me! It's the wrong bowl", bend down and put two spoonfuls of food from the full bowl into the empty bowl. Because the full bowl is in your possession, there is nothing to guard. The dog will polish this small amount off in no time and look up for more. Repeat this procedure until all the food has gone. What is happening from the dog's point of view is that your every approach towards the bowl is to give food and not to take it away.

Next step is to give it a half-full bowl. When it finishes that, you bend down and put the rest in. Progress this stage to putting the rest in, just before the dog finishes the first bit. You are now approaching his trophy, but still with the intention of giving and not taking.

Soon, you will be able to pick up the bowl whilst there is still a small amount of food in it. The dog has learnt that there is still more food around, and you are going to give it to him. During these stages, you will have stood near the bowl whilst the dog has been eating – inside or bordering on the edges of the "forbidden zone". The reason why you will have been able to get away with this is that the dog will also think that he is inside your forbidden zone. We now need to put the food down, leave and re-enter this zone safely.

Place the food on the floor and walk away, but only as far as the fridge where you have left a really juicy titbit. Take it out and walk back towards the bowl watching for any initial warning which will take the form of a freeze posture. Stop if you see this sign and from where you are, throw the titbit into the bowl saying "Here you go. I forgot to put this in." Then walk away. Do not go any closer to the bowl if the dog gives you this warning; otherwise you will have negated any trust that you have built up.

Most dogs quickly accept this departure, return, reward routine. Other members of the family can enter the room whilst the dog is eating, go to the fridge and reward the dog – initially from outside the forbidden zone – but within no time at all they too will be able to enter it and the dog's tail will wag. A random reward basis can then be put into effect.

The tension in this case was very quickly defused and the owner was able to rebuild his dog's trust, just as quickly as he had destroyed it.

Mr and Mrs Flatt are a couple in their mid-40s with no children and a large four-year-old Great Dane called Atlas. Amongst their many problems, Atlas was urinating on their bedroom door, and if he got the chance to get into the room he would urinate on the bed. Atlas actually belonged to Mrs Flatt: he was her dog before she met and married her husband. Atlas used to sleep in the bedroom, but since the wedding had been left in the kitchen at night.

He still regarded himself as the Alpha male, which of course he was until Mr Flatt appeared on the scene. In his eyes, allowing Mr Flatt to occupy the bedroom whilst he was isolated in the kitchen (the furthest room in the house from the bedroom and therefore on the fringe of the pack: the sleeping place of the lowest rank) was on a nightly basis demoting him. For this reason, on a daily basis Atlas needed to reassert his rank. He did this by marking the disputed territory at every opportunity, a perfectly normal canine behaviour designed to signal: "This is my territory. All other males stay away." Mr Flatt was lucky that Atlas did not have the sort of temperament that was prepared to establish his rank through aggression.

During the day, without realising what they were doing, both Mr and Mrs Flatt were allowing Atlas all the privileges of the highest rank and then attempting to demote him at night. This scenario meant that a vicious circle had been created, the start of which was allowing Atlas the privilege in the first place.

The cure was relatively easy to bring about. They had to ensure that Atlas stayed demoted during the day. This was achieved by applying the principles described in Chapter 3. This example shows how dogs view human adults in a permanent pack situation. Any changes in that situation, such as someone going to live elsewhere, or a husband frequently away on business trips, or a newcomer arriving on a permanent basis, will very often result in changes of behaviour which can sometimes reach a problematical level. My colleague, feline behaviourist Peter Neville, defines a behaviour problem as a situation when the joy of owning a pet has been exceeded by the pain of living with it. To the Flatt's, Atlas urinating on the bed had certainly become a pain.

Because they neither wanted to breed from nor show Atlas, they were thinking of having him neutered. This was a course of action suggested to them by one person, whilst another had told them that he was too old for it to make any difference. They wanted to know whether I thought it would cure the problem.

In cases like this, I find that castration on its own does not usually achieve a satisfactory result. His behaviour was more an expression of attitude than a hormonally-influenced problem. However, research conducted in 1970 at the University of Pennsylvania showed a better than 70% improvement in the behaviour of dogs that were castrated, regardless of age. This included research done on dogs of up to twelve years of age, and my own experience with one of our own dogs has proved to me that age is not a factor. Our ten-year-old Weimaraner was suffering from a perineal hernia which sometimes necessitates castration, as it did in his case. He had always been the type of dog who did not welcome the attention of strangers. He did not bother them and openly objected to them bothering him by giving a low growl and sloping off with a suspicious look on his face. He was also a prolific scent marker and anything that was new in the garden always had to be protected from him, otherwise he would mark it when we were not looking. Within a few weeks of the operation, however, other people were commenting upon how gentle he was becoming. His marking activity was noticeably reduced and now, months later, he chooses to approach people and likes being stroked. In short, he is a much nicer dog. All the old wives' tales about castrated dogs getting fatter or becoming sluggish are certainly proving to be untrue in his case. In fact he appears to have a new lease of life.

In 1988, one of my students on the correspondence course that I was commissioned to write for the Canine Studies Institute, Hazel Palmer (now an associate member of the APBC), submitted a survey that she had completed on the effects of surgical castration on problem behaviour in adult dogs. She surveyed 98 dogs of different ages and with different problems, and her results confirmed the American findings. In fact, the message that seems to come through loud and clear is that you only ever get a better dog. By that I mean, castration never makes a problem worse and will quite often improve the behaviour.

When you consider that we do not hesitate to neuter cats, horses, pigs etc. and that the majority of owners choose to have their bitches spayed without a second thought, I do not understand the soul-searching that people go through before they reach a decision about their dogs. Although the majority of vets that I speak to are quite prepared to consider the case for castration as an aid to improving behaviour, some vets are totally opposed to it on the grounds that it is social surgery – an operation carried out for the convenience of owners. I can understand this view, but when I consider the number of dogs being housed daily in the various rescue centres around the country, many of which are the result of unwanted matings, then

I believe that they represent a concrete argument against personal prejudice.

All of this I explained to Mr and Mrs Flatt. I said, "On its own, castration is not the answer. However, if you decide to go ahead with it, you may find that it will help and it will certainly not make him any worse." The Flatts did go ahead and are convinced that it did improve their dog.

I find that once people are in possession of all the facts regarding this relatively simple operation, they are in a better position to make a decision. In general, that decision is to go ahead and have it done and I have yet to hear of one of my clients who has regretted it. In my opinion, neutering a dog is infinitely better than hormone treatment (so called chemical castration), simply because we do not know what long-term effects the hormones might have on the dog. I also think that we are being unfair on our dogs by leaving them entire and denying them opportunity to exercise their natural urges.

DOGS AND DOGS

As a direct descendant of the wolf, the domestic dog is still a predator at heart. Built into this predatory instinct is the knowledge that, if you get injured, you are unable to hunt. If you cannot hunt, you do not eat. If you do not eat, you die. For this reason, almost all displays of dog/dog aggression are usually just for display. Left to the dogs' own devices, very rarely does even the most horrific-looking dog fight result in anything other than minor injuries.

Dogs do not cause fights; people do. As soon as one or other dog shows any sign of aggression, we rush in screaming and shouting. This usually startles the dogs, causing them to display the wrong body postures and initiating the next stage of the interaction which usually takes the form of front feet sparring and teeth fencing (open mouthed, lips back, mouth to mouth contact). This display is frightening to watch and generally causes us to intensify our involvement on the decibel level and even to join in by trying to grab one dog or the other. Again, our involvement interferes with the normal course of events and we push the whole affair another stage forward. This usually causes us to start inflicting pain, either by kicking, punching or hitting with the lead. It is at this stage that the injuries occur, sometimes to one of the dogs but usually to us.

Most of my clients who come to me with so-called dog-aggressive dogs have been injured at one time or another by splitting up what they see as a fight to the death. When I ask what injuries their dog has sustained, they usually report minor ones, if any. When I ask what injuries their dog inflicts on other dogs, they usually report none.

The reason that their dog is likely to come off worse is because most owners grab their own dog first and put them into a vulnerable position.

The theory that turning one's back and walking away from two dogs that are "squaring up" to each other will usually result in a lot of noise but no injury, is very difficult to put into practice. It is even more difficult to explain to poor old Mrs Smith, whose pet Poodle is upside down under your Rottweiler. She is going to take a lot of convincing that the only way that Rottie will close his jaws around her Poodle's throat is if she hits Rottie on the head with her brolly. My records do indeed prove this theory. Very rarely do dogs get seriously injured, quite often people who interfere do.

The vicious circle that is created by owners with a dog-aggressive dog is understandable but quite often heightens the problem. Exercise becomes leash only, and dogs need off-leash exercise for the mental stimulation that it affords. When they see another dog approaching, the owner tightens the lead and decreases the dog's interactive critical distance (as was the case with Donner mentioned in Chapter 7). This tightening of the leash has the effect of lifting the front of the dog into a dominant posture, and represents a threat to the approaching dog. If you are walking your dog across what the approaching dog sees as his territory and your dog is displaying a dominant attitude, there is going to be trouble. What your own dog is probably thinking is: "For goodness' sake, let me drop my head. I'm trespassing and I know it. I do not want to dispute this land claim but you are making me."

Modifying the behaviour of a dog-aggressive dog not only requires careful investigation of its medical background, diet, social status within its pack, effective control etc., it also needs detailed consultation with the owner into exactly how the dog interacts with other dogs and how they inadvertently affect this interaction and therefore usually compound the problem. Above all, it requires instilling confidence into the owner that they are able to handle the problem, which is difficult when other people's dogs are being affected. Most people live with their dog's behaviour until someone else complains. Only then does it become a "behaviour problem".

Dear Mr Fisher,
We have an adult male Ridgeback that is not particularly friendly with other dogs. He doesn't actually fight but he is definitely antisocial with other dogs. We want to get another dog and would like one of the same breed, but we are not really bothered because my wife would quite like a Hungarian Visla. Can you advise us on which breed would be best under the circumstances and how we would go about introducing them. – Mr H., Maidstone, Kent.

I try to steer clear of domestic arguments, especially about which breed scores points over another. Although there are breed specific problems, at the end of the day a dog is still a dog. However, there was clearly no argument involved between this couple. They were trying to make sure that they got it right from the start. My advice on such matters is:

1. Go for whichever breed you decide upon, but make sure that you do not choose one that is similar in temperament, character or attitude to the one you already have. For instance, two males of equal status are going to create difficulties later on because they will constantly try to reach the position of "top dog". This is regardless of how you establish your dominance. Pecking orders are relevant to each individual. Both dogs can see the owner as the leader and accept that fact, but they need to establish where they stand individually within the pack. Whether that battle for status is for Nos 2 and 3, or for Nos 8 and 9 in the pecking order, it will still be highly relevant to themselves. To avoid this problem, it helps to go for a puppy that does not exhibit dominant character traits. It may be a puppy when you pick it, but it is going to grow up and assert itself later.
2. If you own a dog, it helps to pick a bitch as your second dog and the same applies in reverse. Providing you do not want

to breed from them, it is advisable to have them both neutered.

3. If the resident dog is very territorial, then introduce the new dog off territory. This can be done at the breeder's home, or in the garden of a friend. Do not bring a new dog on to the territory of an existing dog for its initial meeting. The bonding of the two will become stronger if the puppy can learn to trust the new adult on a neutral area, before it is educated by that same dog into the rules that apply at home or in the den.

4. If your adult dog chooses to discipline the puppy, do not interfere. Quite often, owners scold the adult for growling or snapping at the puppy. What they do not realise is that at around eighteen to twenty weeks of age, the puppy enters a stage which, in the human, would be equivalent to puberty. The resident dog is therefore going to regard the newcomer as an upstart that needs to learn the rules. If we interfere with this, we are going to create resentment or interfere with the pecking order by raising the status of the upstart and lowering the status of what should be the ranking dog. This pecking order might alter again later when the youngster reaches maturity, and again we should allow it to happen.

Basically, my advice would be similar to the advice that I give to owners who think that they have a dog-aggressive dog. Dogs will be dogs. Let them interact on their level, and there will be no problem. Interfere, and there will be a problem. When introducing a new dog into an established dog/human pack, it is easy to go for a very different type without having to pick a cringing wimp. If you decide to choose otherwise because you particularly want another of the same breed and sex, that's fine, just "Think Dog".

14   Aggression "Problems"

It is very much "in vogue" to attach labels to canine aggression: "territorial aggression", "dominance aggression", "nervous aggression", "pain-associated aggression" etc. Having the type of aggression diagnosed is of no comfort to the person who has just been bitten. A dog bite is a dog bite. It hurts just as much if the dog has bitten because it is dominant, as it does if it is nervous. Obviously, to be able to treat the problem, it is essential that the root cause is determined, but rather than look for *types* of aggression, we should identify the reasons for aggression.

Aggression is by far the most common problem that I deal with. Not because it is the most common behaviour problem that dogs suffer from, but because it is a problem that owners cannot live with. They may tolerate a house-soiling dog, even if it means confining it to the kitchen or the outhouse, but they will not tolerate a dog that is biting them, their friends or strangers.

Understandably, it is also the type of behaviour trait that many people do not like to admit that their dog displays, and some people will go to enormous lengths, especially on the phone, to avoid the real issue.

My wife recently received a call from a lady who said that her dog's problem was chewing. After quite a lengthy phone call, she realised that the owner's answers to her questions were very vague. It was not until she was asked if the chewing was specific, i.e. wood, carpets, furniture etc. that the reason for her vague replies became apparent. Her dog was chewing people.

"You mean, mouthing their hands and arms?" asked Liz.

"Well yes, but the trouble is he draws blood," was the reply. Her dog was biting and she did not want to face up to it, she had convinced herself that all five incidents had happened by accident.

We also get the type of owner for whom ignorance is bliss. The following case history is a classic example.

It started with a phone call which went like this:

"Is that John Fisher?"

Try as I might, I cannot help myself from categorising voices. This voice suggested a Rottweiler owner.

"Yes, speaking."

"My name's Peter . . . is it right that you train dogs?"

"Well sort of. What's the problem?"

"There's no problem mate, I've got this Rottie and he just wants squaring up a bit, you know – training, I mean."

I knew it! After some discussion, he made an appointment to come and see me.

At the agreed time, Peter entered my office accompanied by his wife, Claire, and one of the biggest, fattest, meanest-looking Rottweilers I have ever seen. His name was Bandit. He was 21 months old, and he immediately fixed me with an uncomfortable Rottie stare. The kind that said, "I've heard about you, Fisher, but you have met your match this time."

Peter kicked off the conversation by stating once again that they did not have any *problems* with Bandit. He was just occasionally disobedient.

I asked him what he meant by "disobedient", and was told that he pulled on the lead, did not always come back when called, and had to be shut away when they had visitors because he did not get on all that well with other people.

As you can imagine, this last comment made me feel slightly uncomfortable, especially as, by this time, Bandit was loose in my office and was still staring at me.

What was more to the point, I had noticed that from the moment he entered the room, Bandit had not spared even one glance towards his owners. This usually indicates the dog's total disregard for the status of the owners: they rank way below him. This attitude did not match up with the fact that Peter had reported "no problem", so I asked them some questions about how Bandit behaved under certain circumstances.

"Can you approach his food bowl when he is eating?" I asked.

"What? We can't even get in the same room, but then he does like his food; so I suppose it's fair enough," said Peter.

"You don't see this as a problem?" I asked.

"Not really. I don't like being disturbed when I eat," he said.

"Does he get on your furniture and beds?"

"Yes, he does like his comfort," said Claire.

"And will he get off when you tell him?" I asked.

"Well, we don't tell him to get off. I thought you were supposed to let sleeping dogs lie. He does get cross if we sit on the bed or settee with him, though."

I really could not believe what I was hearing: this couple were living with one of the most dominant, potentially aggressive dogs that I had seen in a long time and they did not know it because they had never challenged him.

Pondering on how best to break the news to them, I leaned back in my chair and made the mistake of crossing my legs. Over the years, I have come to realise that crossing your legs in front of a dominant dog is almost like a challenge. Perhaps it suggests that your raised limb is a prelude to placing it over their withers, as one dominant dog would do to a more submissive rival. All I know is that I have learned not to do it, until I have established the rank to do so.

On this occasion, I forgot. Bandit immediately stiffened, placed his paw on my knee and started to exert a great deal of pressure. To which Claire said: "*Oh look! He likes you.*"

Nothing could have been further from the truth. Without thinking, I had laid down a challenge to Bandit who, from the moment we had met, had been waiting for me to do so. As I was sitting and he was standing. I had no other option than slowly to avert any eye contact with him and just as slowly slide my raised leg back on to the floor. This almost satisfied him. I say almost, because what he did next, pointed me in the direction of how we were going to start to tackle the problems that the owners, as yet, did not realise they had.

Bandit gave a low growl, which travelled up through his body from his tail, circled once and then cocked his leg, depositing a squirt of urine down my trouser leg.

After much discussion, both Peter and Claire agreed to have Bandit neutered as part of a programme to reduce his rank within their environment. This programme obviously could not involve any direct confrontation or strength tests as Bandit would have been more than happy to accept their challenge and reassert his rank.

The advice to have him castrated was given, not just because of his attitude, but also because he occasionally marked territory indoors, always marked territory outdoors and frequently became sexy with cushions and sometimes with Claire. He was clearly overproducing male hormones and I felt that he would become a nicer dog for it. (The pros and cons of neutering are covered in Chapter 13.)

I have since heard from this couple. They reported everything was going to plan and Bandit was becoming much more responsive to them at home and less "disobedient" outside.

In this particular instance, we were able to nip any aggression in the bud. Had it been allowed to blossom, which without doubt it would have done, I would have been dealing with a dog that would have been labelled "Dominant Aggressive". Whatever the label, I am pleased I saw him before the owners recognised a problem and not after.

The causes or reasons for aggression in dogs are varied and almost impossible to list. Except for individual peculiarities, the behavioural approach to solving, or at least controlling, the problem is fairly constant.

There are two areas of aggression where a complete cure is almost impossible, we can only improve the behaviour. One is where the behaviour is genetically acquired, the other – which can also be inherited – is where the dog is nervous.

HEREDITARY CAUSES

The *Concise Oxford Dictionary* describes "Hereditary" as: "Descending by inheritance; transmitted from one generation to another; like, the same as or like what one's parents had."

One of the first things I like to establish when dealing with a case of aggression is the age at which the problem first arose and, if the owners have had the dog since it was a puppy, whether they saw the mother or, better still, the mother and the father.

Whether a problem is genetically inherited or not is very difficult to establish. Problems transmitted through the genes become a permanent and unalterable trait. Surgery can alter physical characteristics but the genes that governed their appearance remain and can eventually be passed on. The same is true of genetically-inherited temperament: the trait is unalterable, but that does not mean that the behaviour is not controllable.

If, as a result of treatment, the behaviour of the dog can be changed to such a point that it no longer has to be controlled, then it is quite likely that the behaviour was not genetically inherited in the first place. Some dogs can inherit the behaviour patterns of their parents through a process of "monkey see, monkey do".

When suspecting genetically-acquired aggression, I always assume that it is learned and advise a behaviour modification programme that is designed to alter alterable traits. One of the comments that many of my clients make is: "We should have known better. We could see that the bitch was aggressive and we should have realised at the time that her pups would turn out the same." Yet, without having access to the bitch, it is imposs- ible to say whether we are initially dealing with a genetically- acquired problem, or learned behaviour. Both are hereditary inasmuch as they are problems that have been passed from one generation to another; the latter is curable, the former only controllable.

Providing the dog was acquired at an early age (around seven weeks), providing the new owners were reasonably knowledge- able, providing the new dog was socialised properly as soon as possible, then usually learned aggression is overcome very quickly. If the dog displays aggressive tendencies later in life, it is almost certainly as a result of some other influence. If all these provisos have been met and the behaviour has remained aggress- ive throughout, then the prognosis is usually that the problem can only be controlled, not eradicated.

Step 1. Restructure of the canine/human pecking order. (See Chapter 3)

Step 2. Use sound aversion to interrupt unwanted behaviour patterns. (See Chapter 6)

Step 3. Use positive reinforcement to encourage desirable behav- iour patterns. (See Chapter 5)

Step 4. Having tackled the pressing issue of aggression, increase general control as a back-up should it be needed – Sit, Down, Stay etc.

These four stages are recommended in all cases of aggression, regardless of the root cause. The only variation would be in the form of additions where there were individual requirements such as diet changes where relevant, or the use of Bach remedies, homoeopathic remedies or veterinary treatment, or the removal of choke chains and the use of broad leather collars or "The Col- leash." (See Pulling in Part 3.)

Treating aggression in dogs is not as simple as merely putting these four stages into operation. Educating the owner on how they should conduct themselves is a vital part of the rehabilitation programme. Quite often, the way in which the owner has behaved in the past can sometimes encourage the dog to become more aggressive. The following scenario will explain.

NERVOUS AGGRESSION

My case notes relating to this particular behavioural problem indicate that the onset is usually caused by a lack of early socialisation. When faced with the real world, the young dog lacks confidence and adopts what the owners read as an aggressive posture. It is at this stage that the owner can influence the future behaviour of the dog for better or for worse. Let us take a look at nervous aggression towards both dogs and people from the aggressor's point of view, and see how the learning process works.

Towards dogs

The owners take their young dog into the park, possibly for the first time and usually on a lead, because they are frightened that it might run away.

They are approached by a large, confident but friendly dog who wants to look over the newcomer. The owners become concerned that their young dog is going to get hurt and start to take avoiding action. The youngster cannot handle the confidence of this strange dog, nor can it run away or show submission because the leash has been tightened and it is being pulled away by the over protective owner. The only other recourse is to raise its hackles, bark and growl. A quick glance would show that all of this is being done in the retreat mode. The ears are back and the dog is trying to put distance between itself and the approaching dog. Dogs recognise these body postures and invariably take the view: "Who wants to play with a weirdo, anyway?" and they go off to find a more sociable playmate. Humans partly recognise the body postures, the fear part and reassure the dog that everything is going to be OK. They try to calm the dog by stroking it and uttering gentle, soothing noises in the same way that they would reassure a frightened child. The dog however takes this as praise for its behaviour: it shows aggression, the owners stroke it and make pleasant noises, and the other dog runs off. It only takes three or four repetitions before the behaviour becomes established. If, however, the young dog was ignored and allowed to interact with the other dog at its own pace, it would learn that there was nothing to be frightened about, and it would become more sociable. Above all, its behaviour would go unrewarded and eventually disappear.

Towards people

Similar circumstances can change a dog that is initially insecure in the presence of strangers into becoming aggressive towards strangers. What should be understood is that the initial interaction might appear to be aggressive, but it is usually just a fear-defence reflex. Defusing the situation is the answer, not inadvertently encouraging the dog.

Whereas other dogs cannot be bothered with a dog that behaves in this manner and usually go away, people tend to want to help and stick around trying to encourage the dog to be friendly. The whole meeting becomes drawn out and traumatic to the dog. Strangers are convinced that if only they can touch the dog, then they will overcome the fear. From the dog's point of view, the attempts to approach are viewed as a threat, while the owner's attempts to reassure are looked upon as: "There's a good dog; that's exactly how I want you to behave." At this stage, most owners can correct their dog by allowing it greater freedom on the lead, asking the stranger to help by ignoring the dog and presenting a slightly sideways posture instead of a frontal and threatening stance, and ignoring the dog themselves so that there is no reward given. By striking up a conversation with the stranger, most dogs will eventually become curious and approach in a hesitant way to investigate. Still the dog should be ignored until it appears more confident, and then a titbit reward can be given by the owner and the stranger should leave. Eventually, titbits can be given to the stranger to give to the dog (after it has approached – not to encourage an approach). This procedure will eventually change the dog's mind about what the presence of a stranger means, the reward is received for the approaching, not for growling and backing off. Curing an older dog requires very firm control over the proceedings by the owner, and a great deal of counselling is necessary beforehand, to ensure that the owner fully understands how to conduct future meetings.

Aggression in dogs is a perfectly normal behaviour; it is the dog's way of expressing its emotions, but in most cases it is used as a defence reflex. Dogs that feel threatened for whatever reason have three choices available to them: Fight, Flight or Freeze. These are referred to as Active Defence Reflexes (ADR) or Passive Defence Reflexes (PDR)

The Freeze reflex is not often seen, but would result in the dog entering a catatonic state when it can no longer control the environmental situation; it is a form of PDR. The most commonly seen reflexes are Fight or Flight.

Some breeds are renowned for their defence reflex, although there are obviously variations within any breed. The Rottweiler and the Jack Russell spring immediately to mind as breeds that exhibit Active Defence Reflexes. The Golden Retriever or the Shetland Sheepdog would in general exhibit Passive Defence Reflexes. If, in the dog's opinion, your actions represent a threat to its safety or well being, one or other of these reflexes will be triggered. A dog with ADR is likely to attack; a dog with PDR is likely to run away, but will still attack if cornered and as a last resort.

If aggression is provoked through the triggering off of one of these reflex reactions, the dog is generally regarded as an aggressive dog. Not so: it is a dog that is showing aggression and that is an entirely different diagnosis. Aggressive situations that arise through reflex reactions can be assumed to have been caused from a lack of trust on the dog's part in what we were about to do. It is this lack of trust that is usually the common denominator in cases of aggression and one of the reasons why I strongly recommend socialisation at the earliest possible age. Properly socialised dogs are confident dogs and confident dogs do not usually bite.

15   Anxiety "Problems"

Behaviour problems can only be loosely categorised. Each case must be examined on an individual basis and the recommended treatment programme should be designed for the individual. It would be no good writing out what was advised for one dog and then giving a copy to every client that has a dog that exhibits similar behaviour patterns. There is no short cut when it comes to modifying problem behaviour.

The only way I do categorise problems is that there are those related to over-dominance and those related to over-attachment. It is into the second group that the majority of anxiety cases would fall.

If aggression is the most common behaviour problem that I deal with, then separation anxiety, especially where it involves destructiveness, must run a close second. Once again, this is not because these are the problems that are most common, but because they are the ones that people have to do something about.

The type of problems that arise through the tension that is created when the owners of these dogs are not with them take various forms – house-soiling; destruction through chewing; destruction with the feet and claws; howling and barking and, in severe cases, self-mutilation. All of these are the dog's outward ways of relieving inner tension, much as humans will pace up and down, smoke, drink or chew finger nails. The problem is usually heightened by the way that owners initially deal with the problem. The dog becomes anxious when left and engages upon some tension relieving behaviour like chewing up Mum's new shoes.

Mum returns home and sees the shoes, scolds or hits the dog. By doing so, she increases the tension and anxiety. Not only is the dog concerned about being left, it is also concerned what will happen when the owner returns. The vicious circle has now been formed and unless it is broken, the problem will get steadily worse.

Whenever I am told about a dog that is exhibiting one or more of these problems, I always ask the same questions.

"Where does the dog sleep?" Invariably, the answer is: "In the bedroom."

"Does the dog follow you from room to room, even trying to get into the toilet with you?" Invariably, the answer is: "Yes."

"What would happen if a door closed on the dog to prevent it from following you?" Usually, I am told: "It will whine and scratch at the door."

"Do you always respond by opening the door?" The answer is usually: "Yes."

"Why does it sleep in the bedroom?" "Because it kicks up such a fuss if it is left in the kitchen", is the normal reply.

Without realising it, the owners cannot leave their dog behind a closed door if they are in the house, and wonder why they have problems when they leave the dog in the house on its own. They have created a situation where, when they are at home, the dog is constantly with them and has freedom of access (on demand) to every room in the house. As a direct result, it cannot stand the desolation of being isolated and will, depending upon the type of dog, lose sphincter control through hyperanxiety; dig at doorways and windows in an attempt to escape; howl or bark like an ostracised wolf; chew on something to relieve the tension or, if it is an introverted type, chew itself, sometimes causing extensive damage. Instead of getting cross with these dogs, my first aim is to get the owners to feel sorry for them.

The successful rehabilitation of these dogs requires a threefold approach.

1. Relief of the anxiety that triggers off the problem.
2. Short term protection of property where destructiveness is involved.
3. Long term restructuring of the environment to give the dog different expectations about what being left alone means.

These are achieved in the following way:

1. I prefer to use either a homoeopathic remedy or one of the Bach remedies to relieve the anxiety. As previously described, these would be relevant to the type of dog that I was treating and would be recommended only after discussion with the referring vet. Most vets are only too willing to try this

approach, usually because they agree with me that the use of
tranquillisers would only mask the problem.

2. House-soiling, damage caused by escape behaviour and
   destructiveness through chewing can all be quickly overcome
   by introducing the dog to an indoor secure kennel. Dogs are
   denning animals: they like corners to sleep in or coffee tables
   to lie under; they make their own dens. When I first suggest
   an indoor kennel, most owners throw up their hands in horror
   because it immediately conjures up pictures of putting their
   dog into a prison. If it is introduced gradually, however, the
   dog regards it as a safe haven. It needs to be something that
   can be made totally secure. (Foldaway show cages can be
   purchased from most pet stores.) Put the cage in the bedroom,
   with the dog's bed inside, together with a bone or some other
   tasty treat. Leave the cage door open so the dog can go in
   and out as it pleases until it regards it as a nice place to be.
   The door can be shut for short periods whilst the dog is
   chewing the bone or asleep.

   Leaving the dog initially for short periods, and without
   having long-drawn-out departures, reassures the dog that
   everything will be all right. Being able to return home,
   knowing that there has been no damage and there will be no
   smelly pile on the carpet (not many dogs will soil their own
   nests) mean that the owner can praise and fuss the dog when
   they return. In this way we can organise a regime of cool
   departures and warm arrivals, whereas in the past the routine
   has generally been one of apologetic warm departures, followed by irate and cold returns.

3. The most important part of the exercise is to get the dog to
   accept separation whilst the owner is in the house. A cooler,
   more detached relationship should be developed. This does
   not mean that the dog should be ignored, but it does mean
   that its access to all areas should start to be restricted. It
   should be understood that the root cause of the problem is
   not how long the dog is left, but that it is left at all. It is the
   fact that the dog is isolated from the owner that needs to be
   worked upon, not the length of time. If the dog whines and
   scratches at a door that happens to get shut on it, and in the
   past the owner has scolded the dog for scratching but still
   allowed it out, then this must be the starting point for the
   environmental changes. The shutting of the door has become

a prelude to the owner returning and telling the dog off, but scratching at the door also brings the reward of getting let out and being allowed to follow. It is all very confusing for the dog. What we need to teach the dog is that having a door shut in its face is a prelude to a pleasurable experience.

My advice to the owner is this. When you want to make yourself a cup of tea or coffee, get up and walk towards the kitchen. At the door, tell the dog firmly to "Stay there" (cold departure).

Shut the door, switch the kettle on, pick up a titbit and return. Praise the dog lavishly, organise a street party for it (warm arrival). The time involved will probably be a matter of a few seconds, but the whole procedure will be different from anything that has ever happened in the past. When the kettle boils, repeat the procedure but do not hang about making the coffee. Switch it off and return to give more reward. It might take three or four repeats before you actually make yourself a drink, but they are all opportunities to organise short term cold departures with warm arrivals. More importantly, they are opportunities to shut the door in your dog's face without it causing a problem.

Within no time at all, this procedure of erratic isolations with variable, but always short, time spans will quickly condition the dog into looking upon having doors shut on it as a very rewarding experience. Eventually, the indoor kennel, which by now should have become the dog's bed, can be moved from the bedroom to the landing. Initially, the bedroom door is left open, but as confidence is built, the door will be shut. The object is to create a variety of "no go" areas within the house and, through this, a less attached relationship between the owner and the dog. It takes time, but the success rate is very high indeed.

Most of my clients come to see me as a last ditch attempt to cure a problem. The fact that they come at all proves to me that they are prepared to work at it. If I can get them to understand that there is a perfectly logical reason why their dog behaves as it does and offer them a solution to their problems, I can guarantee that we are more than halfway towards solving them. Understanding their dogs is what I find most owners really want. Once they understand the relationship from their dog's point of view, their life together can be restructured along different lines.

I have had clients who have broken down in tears when they

have reached the "Ah-Ha" level, and realised that it has been how they have handled the situation that has really caused the problem. Although it is not my intention to make them feel so guilty, I must admit that I get a warm feeling inside when it happens. It proves to me that the relationship between them can only improve and that the Man/Dog relationship will never die out – even if it does now need people involved in my line of work occasionally to prop it up.

16   Games to Play with your Dog

Our dogs are all descended from hunting ancestors and still retain many of those remarkable instincts and senses that they required to seek out prey. This may explain some of the behaviour we consider disobedient during off-lead walks. A dog refusing to come when called can be classed as disobedient. However, look at it from the dog's point of view. A hot trail is so exciting and stimulating to follow that it immediately grabs its attention. You are trying to get him on to a restrictive leash and take him away before he can find out where it leads. You are part of the pack and your dog will not understand why you cannot get excited about this wonderful smell which is pulling at all of his senses. His overwhelming urge is to keep hunting. Your verdict is disobedience.

You know your dog is bright, keen and full of energy. Why is it that you cannot keep his attention and make him obey? Obviously, the previous chapters will give you some indication as to why you are experiencing these problems but let us look at it in another way. Instead of trying to overcome and deny the dog's natural hunting drives, why not use them and make them work for you to increase control and with it the enjoyment of living with your dog?

My involvement with dogs has shown me that it is not enough to feed and exercise them; we must involve ourselves with them as much as we expect them to involve themselves with us. If you can physically and mentally exercise the dog at the same time, your pet will be interested in what you are giving it to do and its attentiveness will increase tremendously.

In general, a dog's greatest asset is the ability to seek out, recognise and follow a specific scent. There are simple games that you can play with your dog which will exercise these extraordinary talents. Stimulating the canine urges will help you to overcome the disobedient attitude.

If you teach your dog these simple exercises with the right

attitude, you will be amazed at the prowess displayed. Your dog will start to look to you for the sort of involvement that stimulates its natural abilities, negating the need to go off and stimulate itself. The result is a more attentive dog and much greater control. A dog which is physically and mentally exercised is a satisfied dog.

GAMES AT HOME

1. Tell your dog to stay or get someone to hold the collar. Show a titbit or toy and pretend to hide it in various places around the room, under cushions, behind chair legs, under carpet corners etc. Leave the titbit in one of these places. Return to the dog and tell him to seek. If necessary, guide him around the room until the idea of the game has been grasped. Give lavish praise on success. Three or four games are sufficient initially and the degree of difficulty can be increased as the dog becomes more proficient. If you are going to give your dog a titbit, it is more fun for both of you to make him find it.
2. Hold on to the dog whilst a member of the family or friend shows a toy or titbit before rushing from the room and hiding. (Make sure the hiding place is not too difficult at first.) As quickly as possible, encourage the dog to find the hidden person, giving the command "Find them". Go with the dog at first, until the game is understood. As soon as the dog discovers the hiding place, both handler and hidden person should give lavish praise, along with the toy or titbit. When the dog is proficient and understands the game and the command, the titbit or toy can be discarded and the dog left to find the person.

Both games can be played in the garden and outbuildings and out walking. Keep the search area small to begin with, and widen it as the dog's expertise and enthusiasm increase. Take care not to over-stretch the dog's ability: otherwise you will lose all the benefits you will gain by teaching it properly.

GAMES IN THE GARDEN

Take a handful of treats, or small dog biscuits, and whilst your dog is watching, either tied up or held by someone, walk around the lawn scattering the treats as though you were feeding chickens. Return quickly to your dog and tell it to "Search". Initially you may have to take it around the lawn on the lead until it understands the game. This type of searching exercise is particularly effective if you have two or more dogs, because they tend to start hunting much more competitively and are consequently more stimulated. I see no reason why our dogs should not have to work for part of their daily food ration in this way. After all, in the wild they would have to hunt before they eat.

GAMES IN THE PARK OR EXERCISE AREA

1. With your dog on a collar and long flexileash, tell it to stay, or get a friend to hold the collar. Show a stick, toy or titbit. Select a specific starting point and direction. Walk away, thirty to fifty yards, scuffing your feet as you go to release more ground scent, leave the reward on the ground and return to your dog along the same route. Tell it to "Track on". Encourage the dog to sniff its way along the same route to the reward. If you find that it wants to run to the spot through memory, increase the distance.

   Have patience until the dog understands. Once he is aware of the command "Track on", and is keen to sniff the ground for your tracks, the distance and direction can be changed.

   Eventually, you should be able to walk a normal scent-trail without scuffing your feet and without your dog seeing you do it but still ending with a reward. It can be up to a distance of a few hundred yards. Go slowly and teach properly.

2. While out walking, and without your dog seeing you, drop a toy in the long grass or behind a tree and continue walking. Attract your dog's attention and encourage him to retrace your route with the words "Look back". (Ten to twenty yards will do to begin with.) Praise success. Use an extending lead, initially to ensure that you can recall the dog on to the trail. When proficiency increases, extend the distance of the lead. Before long, you will be able to send your dog back to find lost keys, a wallet or lead etc.

These games can be played by all members of the family, including children. They are fun for both owner and dog because the owner derives pride from his dog's ability and the dog's working abilities are satisfied. The extra benefit that the owner derives from organising these hunting games is that his rank is increased, as *it is the leader's job to initiate all hunting activity*.

Part III
Problem Solving A to Z

Problem Solving A to Z

It would not be possible to compile a list of every behavioural or training problem; so the following pages are not intended to be a comprehensive behavioural dictionary. They are to be used as an easy guide to some of the more common problems that the average pet owner is faced with. I have already mentioned a variety of different problems in the foregoing pages and where these appear in the list, the reader will be referred to that particular section. Where a problem appears that has not been covered, a brief description of how I would usually deal with it will be given. In this way, I am hoping that the book can also be used as a reference manual to give the reader a starting point on how to set about curing a particular problem, or a different approach if what they are already trying is not achieving the desired results. The following pages are not intended to be read as a chapter because some of the advice on how to cure the problem is obviously repetitive.

ABNORMAL BEHAVIOUR

Most of what we term abnormal behaviour is really just normal canine behaviour exhibited in the wrong place and at the wrong time. Before trying to stop a dog behaving in a particular way, we should first of all ask ourselves: "Is what the dog is doing normal for a dog to do?" If the answer is yes, then we should be planning ways of re-directing the behaviour, not trying to stop it altogether. Stopping what is instinctive is an impossible task. Herding, barking, digging, chasing etc. are all perfectly normal instinctive behaviour, but with some dogs these instincts are accelerated and become a problem to the owner. Usually, more stimulating off-territory exercise improves the situation.

If, however, the behaviour is sudden in onset, especially in an adult dog, then it can be termed as abnormal for that particular dog. We should then be considering recent extrinsic or intrinsic changes that have occurred and which might be influencing the dog's usual behaviour. There might be structure changes in the family: a new baby, someone leaving, long term visitors etc. Perhaps there are changes in the family atmosphere; arguments, illness or bereavement. Job changes may have disturbed the usual routine. Have there been changes in the dog's diet, or possibly in the medical condition of the dog? Has the change followed a season? Is there a bitch in season nearby? All of these factors and many more should all be considered before a course of action can be embarked upon. When dealing with any behavioural problem, it is wise first to put your detective's hat on.

AGGRESSION

See Chapter 14.

ANXIETY

See Chapter 15.

BARKING

Excessive barking can ruin good neighbourly relations, and understandably so. It can also drive the owners to distraction. What triggers off the barking obviously has to be the first consideration. Barking for alarm giving, especially in one of the guarding breeds, is not usually the problem. The problem is that the dog will not stop when the owner arrives. It is normal for a dog to bark as a means of summoning the rest of the pack to help to defend the den. It is the higher ranking animals that should then take over. If the dog will not stop, then the relationship between dog and owner needs to be considered and the techniques described in Chapter 3 should be applied. Sound aversion techniques described in Chapter 6 are useful in these cases. Barking for attention would be treated in the same way.

If the barking is in the owner's absence and more than just alarm barking, it is probably a form of anxiety and Chapter 15 should be consulted. If it is alarm barking, which is usually sporadic, then eliciting the help of the neighbours to use a sound aversive technique can prove not only successful but also a good diplomatic move to show them that you are concerned and prepared to do something. Moving the dog to a quieter place in the house should also be considered.

If the barking is through sheer excitement of some anticipated event – barking in the car on the way to the park for instance – then again the use of sound can be employed to interrupt the noise. Changing the routine and exercise area will also help to change the dog's expectations. Even dummy runs to the park and back without the exercise can help to reduce the excitement. Containing the dog in a car crate, or just securing it in the back by its lead and collar (not on a choke), can also help to reduce this type of barking. Where the barking is through over-excitement, it pays dividends to run through the twelve-point diet questionnaire described in Chapter 9.

BEGGING

This is not usually a problem that I have to deal with. Most owners realise that their dog begs food because they have taught it to do so by giving in to its pleading eyes and salivating jaws in the past. The reason why I have included it is to make the point that you rarely see a dog begging food from another dog. They may watch another eating something, but always from a respectful distance. Possession, especially of food, is nine-tenths of canine law. If the owners have allowed the dog to enter their forbidden zone when they are eating, they are in danger of raising the status of their dog, and other problems might arise as a result.

If it has been allowed to beg in the past, it must stop in the future. Containment during human mealtimes is the easy answer until the dog learns that it does not eat human grade food. If it is not a learned response, then we should consider whether the dog is actually hungry enough to break the canine code that you do not trespass into the eating space of another. If the dog is not absorbing the nutrients from the food that you are giving it, it is going to take liberties at your mealtimes. Diet therapy is the obvious solution (see Chapter 10.) In general, the higher ranking the dog perceives the owner to be, the less likely it is to beg food. Raising the owner's status is described in Chapter 3.

BITING

Why dogs bite is explained in Chapter 14. Puppies bite for an entirely different reason. (See Canine Socialisation 14 to 49 days in Chapter 2.) The needle sharp teeth that they have can hurt humans as well, but instead of smacking them for play biting, we should mimic the reaction that they would get from a litter brother or sister, a high pitched yelp. You will find that on the next occasion they do not bite quite as hard. Gradually, you can teach them not to bite at all. This technique can be applied to all puppies up to around eighteen weeks of age. After that the adult teeth will start to appear and biting takes on a whole new meaning. However gently or playfully they bite then it is meant as a display of dominance which should be discouraged at all costs. Reduction of the dog's rank as described in Chapter 3 will normally overcome the problem.

CAR CRAZY TRAVELLERS

See BARKING in this section.

CHASING

There are two main reasons why dogs chase: one is for fun, and the other is because there is a predatory involvement. Chasing for fun can usually be overcome simply by taking the fun out of it. (See Chapter 6.) Where there is a predatory involvement it is not so easy. The problem usually takes the form of chasing sheep, although chasing horses, cats and squirrels pops up as well. My first enquiry is always, "Can the problem be avoided?" Obviously with sheep chasing this is the easiest and most effective option. If it cannot, then the aversive stimulus must be of the highest kind. First, the status of the owner must be increased. (See Chapter 3.) Next, the Training Discs and the high pitched shrill alarm, described in Chapter 6 are introduced individually on separate days. Once the rank structure has been confirmed and the dog responds to both sound aversion techniques, we take the dog to the sheep on the safety of a flexileash. Both the owner and myself are armed with Discs and a shrill alarm. At the first sign of interest, both shrill alarms are sounded and at the same time one set of Discs is thrown to land in front of the dog. Unless the dog is hightailing back towards us a fraction of a second later, the procedure is repeated. The aversive effect must be instant and is designed to make the dog actually frightened of the sheep. This is not how this form of sound aversion is usually employed, but where the problem involves unavoidable predatorial chasing, then the alternative is that the sheep will be killed and the dog may be shot or put down.

CHEWING

Puppies are going to chew when they start teething so it is important that you get them to accept an indoor kennel from an early age (crate training). This means that you can shut them in when you are not in a position to supervise their activities. Most dogs take quickly to this form of training as they regard the kennel as their den. Then by giving them something to chew on, their needs are satisfied and your furniture is protected. (See Chapter 15.)

What most people do not realise is that some dogs go through *two* teething periods. The first is when the new adult teeth are replacing the puppy teeth. The second is usually between six and twelve months and is caused by the adult teeth settling into the jaw bone. With a few dogs, this can cause quite a lot of discomfort and there will be a physiological need to chew. Once again, the easy answer is crate training and supplying them with a chewable item.

Other causes of chewing can be:
1. Attention seeking. Increase rank and use sound and taste aversion therapy. See Chapters 3, 5 and 6.
2. Diet problems. See Chapter 9.
3. Separation anxiety. See Chapter 15.

DESTRUCTIVENESS

This is usually caused by anxiety. (See Chapter 15.) The advice given for CHEWING (above) would also apply, as would the relevant chapters referred to there. Sometimes, destructive behaviour can also be an indication that there is a dominance problem: "What right does a lower rank have to isolate a higher rank?" What would the managing director of a large company say if the office junior told him to wait in a particular room, and that he would be along in about five minutes because he wanted a word with him? If you are going to isolate your dog, it must see that you have the right to do so, otherwise it is going to complain. (See Chapter 3.)

DIET RELATED PROBLEMS

See Chapters 9 and 10.

DIGGING

This is usually a breed specific behaviour. A Terrier will naturally dig to go to earth. If your Terrier does so, it is a sign that the working instincts are not being stimulated. Chapter 16 will help.

Some dogs will dig cooling holes – generally the northern breeds, Huskies, Malamutes etc. but German Shepherds and Border Collies are not averse to the occasional excavation of the lawn or cabbage patch. Do not leave them out in the garden in hot weather without shade or a cool place to rest. A pregnant bitch might start to dig to provide a den in which to have her pups. Providing a whelping box is the easy answer. A bitch that is having a phantom pregnancy may also dig den-like holes in the garden – and in the carpet or on your settee if given the opportunity! This is a problem that needs referring to your vet. Alternatively, Chapter 11 might be of some use.

The most common cause of digging in the home is generally anxiety related. (See Chapter 15.)

Most dogs enjoy digging. If you have a dog that digs for the sheer fun of it, it is a good idea to provide it with a place to dig. This is not always practical, but if it can be arranged it can limit your dog's digging activities to a specific area. Select an unused area of the garden and take your dog towards it. Tie the dog up and let it see you bury a bone. Encourage the dog to dig it up again. Repeat this procedure once or twice and then occasionally bury a bone when your dog is not looking. Pretty soon you will find that the dog will investigate this area regularly as a possible source of bones. It will also start to use it as a place to bury any bones that you give it and which it does not finish. Its digging instincts will be satisfied.

ESCAPE BEHAVIOUR

The most common form is escaping from the confines of the garden. Some dogs are extremely proficient escape artists. They dig under, go through or go over any barrier that the owner tries to erect. The best cure for this problem is regular supervised exercise and containment at all other times.

The two important factors to consider are:
1. Does the dog have the incentive to escape?
2. Does the dog have the opportunity to escape?

Removing the incentive is difficult. If the neighbour always gives the dog a biscuit when it calls around, it is going to continue to call. The practice of putting the weekly rubbish out in plastic sacks has meant that, for some dogs, Christmas comes round once a week. Lack of mental stimulation too means that some dogs will create their own. More off territory exercise will reduce the need to escape. Also see Chapter 16.

If you wish to remove the opportunity, securing the environment is the first priority. Making fences higher is not as effective as turning the top inwards at a 45 degree angle. If the garden area is large, creating an escape-proof smaller area is another alternative. If this is not practicable, there is a product available called "Invisible Fencing" which is used extensively in the USA. It consists of a wire that is laid a few inches underground and carries a radio signal. The dog wears a special collar that emits a warning buzzer if it goes too close to the boundary where the wire has been laid. If it ignores the buzzer and continues, a mild electric shock is felt. The system is supplied with a training programme, so that the dog learns quickly what the consequences of going too close to the boundary can mean. This lessens the traumatic effect that random shock therapy can have and quickly teaches the dog what causes the unpleasant reaction.

I hasten to add that I am not in favour of electric shock therapy for dogs. However, as in the case of sound aversion therapy described for predatory chasing in this section, the consequences if the dog cannot be stopped by any other means should be taken into consideration. The system is designed for gardens of a quarter of an acre and above. In my opinion it is expensive, but still a fraction of the cost that it would take to fence the same size area. In the past, I have recommended this system to people who own hunting breeds and who live in an area where deer or sheep are prolific in the immediate vicinity. Details are available from: Invisible Fence (Wessex), Westwood House, Bradford Peverell, Dorchester, Dorset DT2 9SE.

Escape behaviour can also be a form of separation anxiety. It would then take the form of damage to carpets near doors, sometimes damage to the door itself, or curtains ripped to pieces when the dog is left, see Chapter 15.

EXCITABLE BEHAVIOUR

I see many dogs that exhibit what the owners incorrectly describe as hyperactivity. If it were true hyperactivity, it would be impossible to control until the root cause had been removed, but excitable dogs are generally dogs that are completely out of control. In almost every case, the dog is calmed down by applying certain rules about how the owners should live with that dog. Naturally, some breeds are more prone than others to excitability – the herding and guarding breeds for example. Nevertheless, the behaviour of the dog should still remain under the control of the owner.

I do, of course, recognise that hyperactivity is a very real problem with some dogs and this will be discussed in the entry for it. My records show, however, that by restructuring the dog's idea of the pecking order, and by the sensible application of positive and negative reinforcement, the majority of "excitable" dogs become less excitable very quickly. The lessons of Chapters 3, 5 and 6 should be applied.

FIGHTING

Dog to dog aggression outside the home is covered in Chapter 13. Where the problem is dog to dog aggression within the home, the problem becomes more difficult to resolve. Usually, by the time I get to see the dogs, they will have been kept apart at home for some time and this will obviously have increased the tension within the environment – not only between the two dogs, but also in the atmosphere around them, with the owners feeling that they are living on a knife edge.

Generally the problem revolves around two dogs, both of which think that they outrank the other. The situation can be exacerbated by the owners who tend to assume the dog that has lived with them the longest should be the top dog. In fact, this is rarely the case. The onset of the problem is usually because the younger or newer dog challenges the other for higher status. Left to their own devices, this can normally be resolved quite quickly, sometimes after only one quick spat. The owners however will not accept that the senior resident should step down, even if it is quite prepared to do so. They scold or hit the challenger and then isolate him to let things cool down. The trouble is that they do not cool down. By punishing and isolating the dog that has probably just established its rank, they have promoted the underdog, and whole business will have to be gone through again. A vicious circle has been created.

Dog fighting for dominance in the home can create a very tense situation, but the less we interfere, the quicker it is resolved providing both dogs are not genetically of equal rank. (See Chapter 2, Human Socialisation.)

If they are both of equal rank, the situation is slightly different. The fighting will persist and will become more and more aggressive. The simplest and safest solution is to find a new home for one of the dogs. This is a decision that many people are not prepared to make, and therefore options are quite limited. If they are both entire males, a solution that has proved successful in the past is to try and establish which of the two dogs might have the rank edge over the other. The dog of slightly lower rank should then be neutered, thus causing a clear cut rank status on a hormonal level. The entire male should then be favoured by the family as the highest ranking. It should be greeted first, fed first, allowed to sleep closer to the owner's bedroom, allowed through doorways first – all of this without giving it the impression that it is higher ranking than the humans. Unfortunately, on too many occasions I see these dogs after both of them have been neutered and obviously they are both still of equal rank. All that can be done then is to try and create a pecking order purely through favouritism.

This situation can also arise with two bitches. It is generally believed that bitch/bitch fighting is the worst kind of dog fight and that they will fight to the death, whereas dogs will not. My experience is that it is no worse than male dog fighting, but I may be wrong. If it is worse, the reason is probably that in the wild only the highest ranking females come into season and the number of them who do is dependent upon the current food supply. (Mother

Nature is a very clever girl.) Bitch fighting is therefore probably a survival instinct: for the survival of their kind.

Although some people do not agree, I have found that a similar programme to the one carried out for equal ranking males has proved to be successful in the past: spay the lower ranking bitch.

FOULING

This is not exactly a behaviour problem, unless it is fouling in the house (see HOUSE-SOILING in this section). The fouling that I refer to is the anti-social off territory fouling. Dog owners are sometimes their own worst enemy. They know what the current feeling is about fouling parks and pavements, yet still there are scores of them who refuse to clear up after their dogs. These people give all dog owners a bad name.

I can fully understand the attitude of those who do not own dogs and sympathise with them. Similarly, I can understand that some dog owners are embarrassed about clearing up after their dogs, especially in crowded places. It is for this reason that I have included the problem in the list. If you do not like to be seen clearing up after your dog, train it to go in an area in the garden before it gets a walk. A lot of people take their dog out so that it can relieve itself and this is the number one priority; the exercise that the dog gets is the secondary consideration. As soon as it performs, the lead is put back on and it is taken home again. Dogs are not stupid, they soon learn that this is the case and if they hang on, the exercise period is longer. If your dog always performs on the way home and not at the start of the walk, think about your motives for taking him out. Just as easily as they can learn not to perform until it is clear that the exercise period has finished, they can learn that the exercise period does not start until they have performed.

If your dog is on a regular diet and fed at regular times, you should be able to predict the times of day when it needs to go out. Take it into the garden, ideally to a specific place and wait. If after ten minutes it has not gone, take it back into the house. Half an hour later, try again. You may need to repeat this procedure a number of times throughout the day. (You can see that time should be put aside to teach it this concept.) Sooner or later it is going to have to go and the moment it does, it should be praised, preferably rewarded with an extra special food treat and then immediately taken for an extra long walk. If, out of habit, the dog happens to go again on the walk, clear it up but ignore the dog. It takes just few days for the dog to realise that if it goes in that particular spot in the garden, it gets a yummy food reward and a nice long walk, but if it goes anywhere else, it is ignored. This procedure is called "Target Training" and most dogs, regardless of age, learn the benefits of hanging on until they reach the target in no time at all.

If your dog goes more than once on a walk, it should be given access to the target area at the end of the walk as well. If it usually goes three or four times on a walk, you should start to consider a diet change.

GUARDING

Guarding Food: See Chapter 13. Dogs and Adults.

Guarding Territory: See Chapters 3 and 6.

Guarding Possessions and toys: The possession of articles (trophying) is a canine way of establishing dominance over others. In this section, under BEGGING, I said that possession was nine-tenths of canine law. I was talking about food at that point, but the same applies to toys and other things like socks, gloves, slippers etc.

Quite often, dogs will pick up an article in the presence of the owner and "dare" them to get it back. This is a clear-cut attempt to dominate, although sometimes it can be done as attention-seeking behaviour. If, when the owner goes to retrieve the article, the dog growls, then dominance is the ulterior motive. See POSSESSIVENESS in this section.

The importance of possessing toys as a means of establishing dominance is well recorded in a book written by my colleague John Rogerson, who is also a member of the Association of Pet Behaviour Consultants (APBC). His book: *Your Dog – Its Development, Behaviour and Training* explains how this urge to possess is a natural process and can be used to give the dominant advantage to the owner.

HOUSE-SOILING

See Chapter 15. If the house-soiling is an overnight problem, and not as a result of an anxiety, the example given in Chapter

7 of the lady who rubbed her dog's nose in the mess that it made is how *not* to cure the problem.

The age of the dog should be taken into consideration. If it is still quite young, the chances are that the problem will cure itself. Most dogs learn naturally to ask to go outside. We can speed up this process by using the Target Training techniques described under FOULING in this section: reward the right behaviour and ignore the rest. Sometimes, if the dog was initially trained through the traditional paper training technique, the fact that paper is still left down suggests to the dog that it is OK to go on it: after all it used to be praised for doing it on paper. Removing the paper, and placing its bed or feed bowls in its place, often stops the habit.

As the puppy gets older, the digestive process alters and so a little bit of diet management can prove useful. For example, if we work on a twelve to fifteen hour digestive process for an adult dog, we can see that feeding at 8 a.m. and 6 p.m. is a sensible routine, providing it has access to the garden before you go to bed. The cycle from one end to the other is relatively shorter in the younger dog, say 8 to 12 hours. We can see that although an 8 a.m. meal is fine, if we feed at 6 p.m. the dog is going to be desperate in the early hours of the morning. During this transitional period from puppy to adulthood, I usually advise owners who have dogs with this overnight problem to make the last feed as late as possible, giving the dog access to the garden shortly after and then bringing the feeding time forward an hour a month. Switching to a high density diet can also help because the dog is being fed less bulk. Crate training as described under CHEWING in this section is also a sensible and effective aid.

HOWLING

See BARKING in this section.

HYPERACTIVITY

This is a very real problem with some dogs, although quite often it is wrongly diagnosed and is really just a lack of effective control. See EXCITABLE BEHAVIOUR in this section.

Real hyperactivity results in the dog not being able to control itself and therefore not being able to learn – much like a hyperactive child. There are various causes, and usually some detective work is required on a trial and error basis. I find the biggest culprit is diet. (See Chapters 9 and 10.) There can be other reasons and I have had cases where changing the drinking water, changing the feed bowls, stopping certain titbits etc. have resulted in the dog becoming calmer and more manageable. If you suspect hyperactivity and you have tried the suggestions given for excitement with no results, then you will have to go on to the trial and error trail. A good place to start is with the low protein natural diet advised in Chapter 10.

Puppy-farm dogs, and dogs that have been reared from a very early age by humans (two to three weeks of age or earlier), can sometimes exhibit hyperactive behaviour. The dog's activity level is variable throughout a twenty-four hour period, whereas a cat is at its most active at night and humans by day (or should be). I have known a few cases of hand-reared puppies taking on the activity level of the human and not resting at all during the day. Recently, I have been having a great deal of success with truly hyperactive dogs by using a Vitamin/Mineral/Amino Acid supplement called Serene-Um (available in many pet shops and marketed by a company called Mark and Chappel). It is formulated for hyperactive and/or aggressive dogs and cats. As it contains ingredients of natural origin, it can do no harm and quite often is very helpful.

JOGGERS

See CHASING in this section.

JUMPING UP

This is a highly social and usually dominant way for dogs to say "hello". Similar behaviour can be seen between two dogs, the more submissive type being the one that is jumped upon. How must it appear to the dog if we allow it to jump all over us? The behaviour starts as a puppy and takes the form of a food soliciting greeting: wolf cubs greet the returning adults by lip licking as a way of getting them to regurgitate food. The purpose of jumping on humans is to reach our faces, instinctively for the same reason. Just as puppy biting is an instinctive behaviour (see BITING in this section), then so is jumping up. When play biting takes on a different meaning, then so does jumping up. If we do not recognise the learning effect that this must have on a young dog and allow it to continue in the hope that it will grow out of it, then we allow our dogs to dominate us and our visitors without realising it. Freedom of movement through the entrance to our den should be under the control of the highest ranking animal. If your dog pushes past you and jumps all over your visitor, you should start to question your relationship with your dog. See Chapter 3.

The simple solution, after you have established a consistent rank structure, is to interrupt all learned behaviour (see Chapter 6), and to establish an alternative form of greeting. Teaching the dog to sit means that it cannot jump up, as its bum is on the ground. (See Chapter 5). Forget the old wives' tales that you knee the dog in the chest, stomp on its back feet, squeeze the front feet etc. Increasing your rank, interrupting learned behaviour, and offering a more rewarding alternative quickly cures this problem.

LICKING

Dogs do not lick humans because they like the salt on our skin. Licking usually occurs with small puppies and generally the more submissive types. The truth of the matter is that some humans are actually flattered by the puppy's display of affection and encourage the behaviour by not discouraging it. Because we read it as a display of affection, we usually respond by returning the affection in the form of soothing words and gentle strokes. If we are not careful, we are in danger of turning a submissive gesture into a dominant gesture. Because we respond so readily, we can quickly teach the rapidly developing young dog that it is an ideal way of gaining our attention. In the same way, a young child that is a little horror can turn on the cute baby talk and quickly achieve an aaah! response from a maternal person.

We need to establish whether the behaviour is attention seeking or a submissive gesture. A simple way of doing this is to ask yourself the question: "Does my dog lick me when I am doing something else, or does the licking occur after I have spoken to or stroked the dog?" In other words, which one of you initiates the interaction? If it is a submissive display, a less dominant form of greeting should be used by you. Crouching down to praise is less dominant then leaning over. Stroking the side of the cheeks and gently patting the flanks is less dominant than stroking the head, neck and shoulders. It also helps to reduce the amount of physical contact for a short while and substitute verbal praise instead. If the licking is initiated by the dog, it is almost certainly attention seeking and the danger is that it could be turned to the dog's advantage in the constant battle for pecking order. (See Chapter 3.)

Sound aversion therapy is also useful to interrupt the behaviour without giving a reward. (See Chapter 6.)

MOUNTING

In both dogs and bitches, this is behaviour very similar to jumping up. The placing of the paws on another animal is a dominant gesture, but it is seen most frequently in the male. It is not unusual to see a young male of five to six months of age trying to mount people's legs or cushions etc. and engaging in pelvic thrusts. This usually indicates changes in the hormonal status of the dog consistent with the onset of puberty. Usually the dog will grow out of the habit but if it persists in the adult dog, then it can become very embarrassing to the owner to say nothing of the embarrassment caused to the person being mounted. If the dog is also a prolific sniffer and scent marker, (see TERRITORY MARKING in this section) then veterinary advice should be sought on the possibilities of neutering. In most cases this successfully cures the problem. In the absence of other clues that the behaviour is hormonally induced, then it more than likely is an attempt to dominate. Reducing the dog's rank (see Chapter 3) and sound aversion therapy (see Chapter 6) normally cures the problem.

MOUTHING

See BITING in this section. Also see Chapter 3.

NERVOUSNESS

Treating and improving the nervous behaviour of dogs is very rewarding. We humans feel very sorry for a nervous dog, yet we seldom feel sorry for an aggressive dog. However, the two conditions are very closely linked and therefore the treatment programme is similar. (See Nervous Aggression in Chapter 12.) With nervous dogs, it is usually quite common to find all sorts of diet-related clues. This is an area that I generally explore in great depth. (See Chapter 9). After consulting the referring vet, I usually find that one of the homoeopathic or Bach remedies can be extremely useful in such cases. (See Chapter 11.)

POSSESSIVENESS

Dogs who are possessive of toys, beds and stolen articles like socks or slippers are normally dominant or leader dogs. Without realising it, you actually encourage this behaviour with early games of tug-of-war or chase games for fun when the puppy picks up one of your socks. Taking a toy or article of any kind into its sleeping area and challenging you to stay away from it is a way of establishing dominance over you. Sound aversion therapy and not direct confrontation is the best way of controlling the behaviour. (See Chapter 6.) Establishing your leader role is the best way of ensuring that the behaviour does not arise at all. (See Chapter 3.)

PULLING

Pulling on the lead is probably the one consistent trait exhibited by all dogs that have a problem related to over dominance. Most of my clients have attended some sort of formal training with their dogs, yet their dogs still pull them from A to B. In the long run, the cure must be to take away the attitude that tells the dog that it must walk ahead of the owner. (See Chapter 3.) Short term, we need an effective means of stopping the pulling. I am against the use of choke-chains because, unless you are a skilled dog trainer, I find that they do not work.

In far too many cases, my clients arrive with their dog wearing a choke-chain and pulling like a train. On investigation of the neck, we find damage to the hair and skin tissue. Dogs who do not respond almost immediately to the correct use of this piece of equipment continue to pull their owners just as much as they would on a broad leather collar. The difference is that the choke-chain tightens around the neck and will eventually cause muscle and tissue damage.

My main objection to choke-chains is that although they are on sale in most pet shops there are no instructions given on how to fit one, or on how to use one. The sad fact is that because of the television programmes that have been done on dog training, the majority of owners genuinely believe that this is the way to stop a dog pulling. In fact, not only does it not stop pulling in most cases, it actually increases some behavioural problems.

In fact, I am against any form of restraint that uses pressure, either on the neck through the use of choke or slip collars, or across the bridge of the nose through the use of the head collars that are on the market. These rely on leading the dog from under the bottom jaw, thus increasing the pressure on the top of the nose.

For this reason, I have developed a collar and lead combined called the Col-leash. The major differences between this and other similar looking collars are:

1. Once fitted comfortably on the dog, there is a locking clip that prevents any part of it from tightening on any part of the dog's head.
2. The dog is led from a point on the side of the neck just below the ear. This is the point of least resistance. It means that there is no way that the dog can adjust the position of its head to form a straight line through which it can pull.
3. The Col-leash is fully adjustable to fit most dogs; so there is no danger of getting the wrong size.

My reason for designing the Col-leash was that it is important when applying the principles set out in Chapter 3, that the dog should not be able to regain its rank by being able to pull or lead the owner. The Col-leash has a very high acceptance rate with dogs who struggle and resist any other form of control. It enables owners to walk with their dogs at heel without the use of strength and it enables dogs to display normal body and head postures. The dog's front end is not being pulled up into a dominant posture, which happens with neck restraints; and the head is not being forced into a submissive posture, which happens with nose restraints.

If the Col-leash is fitted on a puppy as its first lead, it never learns to pull at all and this in itself prevents all sorts of problems. As it is a one size adjustable piece of equipment, it will grow with the pup, and the owner does not have to keep paying out for bigger and bigger sizes. It is available from the main distributors: Alan and Piers Pet Products, Crowhall Farm, Northfield Road, Soham, Near Ely, Cambridgeshire, CB7 5UF.

RECALL

This is probably the hardest lesson for the dog to learn, because disobedience here is self rewarding. Owners who have recall problems with their dogs actually increase the problem by putting them on the lead the moment they are able to catch them, invariably telling the dogs off as they do so and then taking them home. Not coming back means that the dog can continue to have fun, coming back means that it cannot. (See Chapter 5.)

A method that has proved successful in the past is to teach the dog some new expectations about what going home means. The idea is to split the daily food ration into as many equal portions as the dog has walks in a day. If the dog has only one walk a day, it is as well to increase this to three or four shorter walks. For about a week, the dog is walked on the safety of a long line or Flexi-leash. Once it arrives back home a portion of its daily food ration is given. Most dogs quickly learn that they get fed at the end of a walk, and this gives them a good reason for wanting to come back to the owner. When off-leash activity is resumed, it is sensible to exercise the dog on new territory for the first three or four occasions. The natural instinct to keep close together as a pack on fresh terrain comes into play and allows the owner the opportunity of practising the recall response from a free running dog.

With particularly resistant dogs, feeding them when they get home is not enough incentive. Taking their portion of food to the exercise area usually does the trick as the dog views its food entirely different to the way that it views titbits. The ultimate responsibility of keeping the pack together rests with the leader; so owners with dogs who exhibit this problem behaviour must examine their own role in the pack structure. (See Chapter 3.)

STOOL EATING

This behaviour is called Coprophagia. Although strictly speaking it is a behaviour that your vet would normally advise you on, I have included it in this list because so many of my clients mention that their dogs do it as a secondary problem to the one they are consulting me about. First of all, this is perfectly normal behaviour for dogs, especially puppies. When they are very young and still with their mothers, mum would eat the puppies' faeces to keep the nest and surrounding area clean. Some puppies pick up this habit through a process of "monkey see, monkey do".

Sometimes the habit persists but usually dies out as they get older. There are a number of other reasons why some dogs eat their own stools; so in all cases of this behaviour occurring in an adult dog I advise the owners to seek veterinary advice, to make sure that there is no pancreatic or other medical condition that is causing the problem.

Excessive punishment for puppy accidents, or house-soiling as a result of anxiety, can teach the dog that the combination of a pile on the carpet and a human in the room is bad news and, as a result, they eat their own faeces to eliminate part of this combination. (See Chapter 15.)

A mal-absorption problem, which means that the food is not being properly digested, would be quickly spotted by your vet, but sometimes the diet itself is of poor quality or not correctly balanced, and the dog is not able to extract the right nutrients from it. This is not so easy to spot. Short term diet therapy is usually successful if this is the case. (See Chapters 9 and 10.) In all but a very few cases, this behaviour can be quickly overcome providing, just as with any other problems, the root cause can be established first.

TERRITORY MARKING

By far the biggest culprit in this category is the male dog that lives with a female owner for a period of time on his own and then another human male appears on the scene. This scenario, or a version of it, crops up time after time where territory marking is the reported problem. Any situation where the male dog has been given the role of Alpha male, with no other male around to challenge that rank for a period in excess of about fourteen days, is likely to start territory marking activity if another male appears on the scene. I find that asking the client to draw a brief sketch of the layout of the rooms, indicating the places where he is most likely to cock his leg, gives me an indication of where to start the investigation process. Invariably, the territory marked is the master bedroom. (See Chapter 13, Dogs and adults.)

Sometimes the behaviour is hormone related. If you suspect this, you should ask your vet whether neutering will help. Dogs that are constantly sniffing and drooling over smells outside, and that constantly mark territory wherever they are, usually benefit from castration.

In most cases, I find the root cause is a change in the environment that the dog views as a threat to his rank: new baby on the scene perhaps, or a new grandchild that is regularly brought to visit and takes the attention off the dog. Where this is the case, the root cause is in how the dog perceives his role in the environment. Restructuring the pecking order usually cures the problem. (See Chapter 3.)

Visitors

Nearly all of my clients who complain about behaviour problems that can be attributed to over dominance, as opposed to the problems that are attributed to over attachment, also complain about the dog's attitude to visitors. These dogs are either aggressive to visitors or over friendly towards them to a point where the dog has to be shut away when visitors call. This adds to the problem. From the dog's point of view, if every time someone called, isolation to another part of the house became automatic, then it would be a good idea to drive the visitor away (aggression), or to stop them coming in (over exuberance). Either way, the answer is the same: increase the rank of the owner so that they make the decision about who does and who does not have freedom of access through the doorway, and interrupt all learned behaviour. (See Chapters 3 and 6.)

Appendix
Case Statistics

During the time it has taken to write this book – and knowing that within its pages I would be stressing the importance of diet, proper early socialisation, the effects of traditional training attitudes etc. – I have collated all the information on the dogs that were referred to me over this period. The purpose of this was to produce some statistics which would turn the words between the covers into hard facts. The figures that follow have been collected from the case notes of 468 dogs, involving 67 different breeds and who together exhibited 620 behaviour or training problems.

I knew that by the time I had written the last page of the book, my figures would confirm what I had written within its chapters. The percentages at the bottom of the chart show this to be true.

What I was not to know was that during the time of writing, the Rottweiler would receive more and more bad publicity. Again, the figures show the true facts – they are not the bad breed that the media have made them out to be.

BREED TYPE	Problems of treatment			General lack of control often described as hyperactivity			Anxiety related problems			Specific sexual behaviour
	Aggression to people	Aggression to dogs	Nervous behaviour	Jumping up	Recall	Pulling	Destructive behaviour	House-soiling	Howling and barking	Excessive mounting behaviour
Airedale		1		1	1	2	1			
American Pit Bull		1								
Australian Terrier					1					
Basset Hound	1									
Beagle				1	2	1				
Belgian Shepherd	2	1		1	1	2				
Bernese Mountain Dog	1		3	2	2	2				
Bichon Frisé								1		
Blood Hound				1	1			1		
Border Terrier	1	1								
Boxer		1	1	1	1	1				
Briard	1			1	1	1				
Bull Dog	1									
Bull Mastiff				2	2	2				
Cav. King Charles	1	1	3				3	6	4	1
Chinese Crested Dog	1									
Chow Chow	1									
Cocker Spaniel	7	3		2	2	2	2	2	1	1
Collie – Bearded				1	2	1				
– Border	5	5	1	6	6	9	4	5	1	
– Rough	1	1	2					1		
Corgi							2		1	
Cross Breeds	11	17	2	11	14	12		5	1	6
Dacshund	1							3	1	
Dalmatian			1			1	1	2		
Deer Hound		2								
Dobermann	5	7		1	3	2	1	1		
English Bull Terrier										
Flat Coated Retriever							2			
Fox Terrier				1	1	1	1	1	1	
German Shepherd Dog	18	19	3	15	18	22	2		2	
German S/Hair Pointer		2						1		
Golden Retriever	7	3		4	6	6	1	2		
Great Dane	1	2		2	2	2		1	1	
Hova Wart		1		1	1	1				
Irish Setter	1			2	2	2				
Irish Wolfhound	1	1								
Italian Greyhound					1			1		
Jack Russell	2	2					1		1	1

Specific fear	Specific over-excitement	Specific aggression								
Phobic behaviour	Car crazy	Food guarding	Number of breed seen	Rescue dog	Via dealer or puppy farm	Evidence of diet problem	Obtained after 14 weeks kennelosis	Total % of diet related problems	Total % of rescue/puppy farm & kennelosis dogs	Had some formal training
1			5			1		20%		2
			1							
			1			1		100%		
			1			1	1	100%	100%	
			2							1
1			3	1		2	2	66%	100%	2
			4			2	1	50%	25%	
			1							
			2							1
			2		1				50%	1
			3	1	1	2		66⅔%	66⅔%	3
			2			1		50%		
			1							
			2			1	1	50%	50%	1
3		1	19		2	9	1	47.3%	15.7%	6
			1							
1			2				1		50%	
		8	26		4	5	3	19.2%	26.9%	18
1			3	1		2		66⅔%	33⅓%	2
1	1		35	3	2	10	4	28.5%	25.7%	22
1			5			1		20%		3
	1		3			1		33⅓%		1
2	1		71	21		18		25.3%	29.5%	48
			5			2	2	40%	40%	
			5			2	1	40%	20%	3
			2				1		50%	
			17	3		9	3	52.9%	35.2%	12
1			1							
			2			1		50%		2
			3							
2			63	10	3	25	5	39.6%	63.4%	45
			3	1		1		33⅓%	33⅓%	1
		2	27	1	6	8	4	29.6%	40.7%	14
	1		9			1		11%		5
			1							1
			3	1		3	1	100%	66⅔%	1
			2				1		50%	1
	1		2							
1			7							3

BREED TYPE	Problems of treatment			General lack of control often described as hyperactivity			Anxiety related problems			Specific sexual behaviour
	Aggression to people	Aggression to dogs	Nervous behaviour	Jumping up	Recall	Pulling	Destructive behaviour	House-soiling	Howling and barking	Excessive mounting behaviour
Keeshond				1	1	1				1
Labrador	1	4	1	6	6	7				
Lakeland Terrier									1	
Lancashire Heeler				1				1		
Lhasa Apso								1	1	
Lurcher						1		1		
Munsterlander	1									
Old English Sheepdog	1			1	1	1	1			
Patterdale Terrier										
Poodle – Miniature	1			1	1					
– Standard								1		
Puli		1	1							
Pyrenean Mountain Dog	1									
Rottweiler	4	2	1	5	6	4		1		
Saint Bernard	1									
Saluki	1				2					
Samoyed	1			1	1	1			1	
Schnauzer – Miniature				1	1				2	1
– Giant	1									
Sealyham					1					
Shihtzu					1			1		
Springer Spaniel	2		1	4	8	6				
Shar Pei	1									
Staff. Bull Terrier	2					3	1			1
Tibetan Terrier								1	1	1
Weimaraner	1	3		1	2	2				
West Highland Terrier	2	1			1				2	1
Yorkshire Terrier									3	1
67 Breeds	91 19.4%	82 17.5%	20 4.2%	77 16.4%	103 22%	98 20.9%	27 5.7%	46 9.8%	19 4%	13 2.7%

Aggression to people includes owners and children but does not include specific aggression such as food guarding.

Aggression to dogs includes Dog/Dog Bitch/Bitch aggression at home.

Some dogs exhibit more than one behaviour problem.

The diet figures do not necessarily mean that this was a diet related behaviour problem – just that after checking against my usual 12 point check list, there was evidence that the dog's usual diet was unsuitable in some way.

Phobic behaviour (Specific fear)	Car crazy (Specific over-excitement)	Food guarding (Specific aggression)	Number of breed seen	Rescue dog	Via dealer or puppy farm	Evidence of diet problem	Obtained after 14 weeks kennelosis	Total % of diet related problems	Total % of rescue/puppy farm & kennelosis dogs	Had some formal training
	1		3			1		33⅓%		1
1	1		17		2	6		35.2%	11.7%	10
2			3			2	1	66⅔%	33⅓%	1
			1				1		100%	
			2							
			2							1
			1							1
		1	5		1	1		20%	20%	2
1			1			1		100%		1
			2							
			1							1
			1			1	1	100%	100%	
			1							
2		1	20	1	1	3	1	15%	15%	14
			1							
			3							1
			3	1	1	2		66⅔%	66⅔%	2
			4							1
			1							1
			1				1		100%	
1			3							
	1		15	2	1	7	1	46.6%	57.1%	11
			1							
1			8							4
			2		1	1		50%	50%	
			7			4		57.4%		4
			8		4	2	1	25%	62.5%	3
			4		1	4	1	100%	50%	1
23 4.9%	8 1.7%	13 2.7%	468 dogs exhibiting a total of 620 problems	47 10%	31 6.6%	144 30.7%	42 8.9%			259

Total problems related to lack of early experience/rescue	25.6%
Total of unsuitable diet cases	30.7%
Total of dogs who have had formal private/dog club training	55.3%